TO

_____

FROM

_____

DATE

_____

★ ★ ★

Huddle Up! 40 Sport Devotions for Coaches and Parents of Little Athletes
Copyright © 2018 by Mark Gilroy Creative, LLC
www.markgilroy.com
First Edition, March 2018

Published by:

P.O. Box 1010
Siloam Springs, AR 72761
dayspring.com

Bible verses were taken from the following translations:

Scripture quotations marked CEV are taken from the Contemporary English Version. © 1991, 1992, 1995 by American Bible Society. Used by permission.

Scripture quotations marked ERV are taken from the Easy-to-Read Version, © 1993 by the Bible League International. Used by permission.

Scripture quotations marked ESV are taken from The Holy Bible, English Standard Version®, copyright © 2001 by Crossway, a publishing ministry of Good News Publishers. Used by permission. All rights reserved

Scripture quotations marked NIRV are taken from the Holy Bible, New International Reader's Version®, NIrV® Copyright © 1995, 1996, 1998, 2014 by Biblica, Inc.™ Used by permission of Zondervan. All rights reserved worldwide.

Scripture quotations marked NKJV are taken from the New King James Version®. Copyright © 1982 by Thomas Nelson. Used by permission. All rights reserved.

Scripture quotations marked NLT are taken from the Holy Bible, New Living Translation, copyright © 1996, 2004, 2007, 2013, 2015 by Tyndale House Foundation. Used by permission of Tyndale House Publishers, Inc., Carol Stream, Illinois 60188. All rights reserved.

Scripture quotations marked TLB are taken from © The Living Bible. Taken from the Living Bible with permission from Tyndale House Publishers, Inc., Wheaton, IL.

Written by Mark Gilroy
Cover Design by Gearbox (studiogearbox.com)

Printed in China

Prime: 71934

ISBN: 978-1-68408-225-4

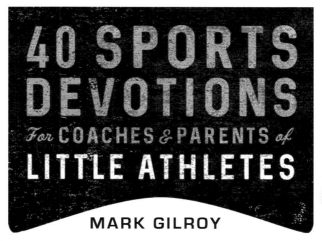

HUDDLE UP

40 SPORTS DEVOTIONS
For COACHES & PARENTS of
LITTLE ATHLETES

MARK GILROY

FORWARD BY MIKE MATHENY
Manager of the St. Louis Cardinals
and Best-Selling Author

CONTENTS

THE RIGHT TEAM

FORWARD

My Christian faith has been the guiding principle of my life as a player and manager. I'm so grateful for parents and coaches who have encouraged me in my personal walk of faith. That's why I am so delighted to endorse *Huddle Up!*

When our children huddle up with God, they learn so many important lessons in life: faith, teamwork, preparation, resilience, discipline, how to handle defeat and success, goal-setting, trusting others, hard work, and the simple pleasure of doing one's best.

If you are a parent reading this, the greatest encouragement you can give your young athlete is the "strong, silent support" that shows you trust that God has put your child with the right coach and the right team at the right time. No game or season will be perfect, but give your son or daughter the space they need to learn the lessons that God has prepared for them. Most of all support your child and their coach with prayer.

If you are a coach reading this, thank you for your commitment to providing a fun, positive, skill- and character-building experience for our young people. Like me, I'm sure you can think back to the coaches and other adults who helped you grow up and grow stronger in your faith. You have a great opportunity to be that same kind of influence to a young person this season. Compete hard, teach hard, but most of all, pray hard for the children God has entrusted to you.

When we huddle up as parents, coaches, and young athletes, we come together to reaffirm our strategies, our plans, our goals, and most of all our belief that God knows us, loves us, and has wonderful plans for our lives.

That's always the right team!

– Mike Matheny
Manager, St. Louis Cardinals and
author of NY Times best-selling
book *The Matheny Manifesto*

———————————

"I love it when coaches look at sports as a way to mentor young athletes in character development, which is the real reason we play the game. *Huddle Up!* is a great resource to help both adult supporters and youth participants keep their focus on what matters most, becoming exceptional men and women of faith, character, and values."

– Tommy Kyle,
Executive Director
of Nations of Coaches

"For many of us, playing sports was our most passionate endeavor as we grew up. I absolutely love how *Huddle Up!* weaves lessons on faith, life, and sports to help young people keep their eyes on the real prize—loving and serving Jesus Christ."

– Collin Klein,
**Heisman Trophy finalist
and Quarterback Coach,
Kansas State University**

INTRODUCTION

WELCOME TO HUDDLE UP!

Do you love playing sports? Do you love being on a team? If you answered yes, then you are going to love *Huddle Up!*

It is filled with short stories that tell about what kids like you have experienced on their team.

Sometimes we win a game and sometimes we lose a game, but *Huddle Up!* helps us to be winners in life. Not only does it share great stories from sports, but it also teaches us important principles from the Bible.

When we follow God's Word, we grow closer to Jesus and learn to do the right things. We get encouraged so we can do even better in sports and in every other area of life.

Are you ready to *Huddle Up*? Read on. There are some great stories written just for you!

Get ready to grow closer to God!

A NOTE TO PARENTS AND COACHES

FUN WAYS TO HUDDLE UP!

Huddle Up! is a great resource to help young athletes grow closer to God.

Huddle Up! is perfect for you as coach to use before or after practice or on a road trip with your entire team. The devotional stories will help you and your young athletes relate faith in God with the sport they love so much.

Huddle Up! also works great for family devotions. The stories provide you as a parent opportunities to discuss how your child can give their best in sports—but more importantly in their faith. Families that pray together grow stronger together!

Huddle Up! can be used by children who are readers. They will love to learn about other kids who have experienced the same things that they have in sports. Most of all, they will learn that the Bible applies to every area of life, including sports.

What's the best way for YOU to *Huddle Up* with your young athletes?

A PERFECT DOUBLE PLAY

WHAT HAPPENS WHEN YOU DON'T GET TO PLAY YOUR FAVORITE POSITION?

Since he started playing T-ball, Zackary had played shortstop on every team he was on. He loved scooping up ground balls and making the throw to first place. And Zack was a very good shortstop. He almost never let a ball go between his legs into the outfield. In first, second, third, and fourth grades, Jack was always his team's shortstop.

The summer before fifth grade, Zach moved up to a new league and a new team, the Blue Sharks. He really liked his new coach and teammates, but was a disappointed when he learned that the Blue Sharks already had a shortstop. His name was Jack. Zack was sent out by the coach to play second base.

Zack tried not to be upset, but it didn't seem fair. He should at least get a chance to show how good he was. Zack wondered if he should talk to the coach after practice and ask if he could have a turn to try out for shortstop. But after watching Jack field hard ground balls, Zack had to admit, Jack was the best shortstop he had ever played with or against. No way could he beat Jack for the job.

On the drive home after practice, Zack's mom noticed that he was very quiet. He was just staring out the window at cars driving the other direction.

"What's wrong, Zacky?" she asked.

Zack didn't like being called Zacky and was glad none of his friends or teammates were around to hear that name. He thought they might tease him.

"Nothing," he answered.

"Are you sure?" his mom asked. "It looks like something is bothering you. Did something bad happen at practice tonight?"

"No. But I don't think I'm going to get to play shortstop for the Blue Sharks," he said

"Why not?" Mom asked.

"There's another kid. His name is Jack. And he's really, really good."

"Well, you're very good, too, Zacky," she said.

"But not as good as him," Zack said glumly. "Not by a long shot."

"So you're not going to get to play?" she asked her son with concern.

"Yes, but I'm playing second base," Zack answered.

"What's wrong with second base?" she asked.

"It's not shortstop. The best infielder is always the shortstop."

"It sounds like Jack is the best infielder," she said softly.

"He is."

"Does that make your team better?" she asked.

"Yes," Zack answered with a frown.

"Then you should be happy. Every good team

has a good second baseman, too, right?"

Two weeks went by and the first game of the season arrived. The Blue Sharks were playing the Tigers. It was a very close game. When the Tigers came up to bat in the last inning, the Blue Sharks were ahead 6–5. They had to get three outs to win the game.

With one out and the bases loaded, the Tigers' best batter came to the plate. He swung hard at the first pitch and missed it.

We have to get this out, Zack thought to himself. He was nervous but stayed on his toes, ready for anything.

With a full count, the Tiger hit a hard shot up the middle of the diamond. Zack knew there was no way he could get to it. But then he saw Jack dive for the ball and nab it in his glove. Jack jumped to his feet and quickly tossed the ball to Zack, who stepped on second place and threw as hard as he could to first base. The first baseman caught the ball just before the Tiger stepped on first base. It was a double play. The Blue Sharks won!

As Zack trotted in to celebrate with his new teammates, the coach was beaming with pride.

"Great play, boys," he shouted. "That was a beautiful Jack and Zack double play!"

He and Jack gave each other a high five. Second base was going to be a lot of fun, Zack thought with a smile.

LIFE LESSON

Sometimes we get sad and maybe a little mad when we don't get exactly what we want. But if we keep a great attitude, if we stay positive, and if we are humble, we will discover there is still so much to be happy about in life.

VERSE TO REMEMBER

In whatever you do, don't let selfishness or pride be your guide. Be humble, and honor others more than yourselves. PHILIPPIANS 2:3 ERV

TO TALK ABOUT

How should we act when we don't get our way?

THE RIGHT CALL

WINNING FEELS GREAT, BUT DOING THE RIGHT THING FEELS EVEN BETTER!

Devan ran as fast as she could to the side of the court, stretched out her racquet as far as she could, and somehow managed to hit the tennis ball back over the net. The point kept going. She and Jeana were playing for first place in the city tournament. They were good friends but still had to play against each other in tennis matches. Sometimes Devan won; sometimes Jeana won.

This was a particularly tough match. The first set, Devan won when she hit a backhand shot across the court that Jeana couldn't get to. Jeana won the second shot with a hard serve that Devan hit into the bottom of the net.

Now they were fighting for every point in the final and deciding set. When Jeana hit a great serve to win a game and take a 5–4 lead in games, Devan knew that she had to win the next game or the set and match would be over. Jeana would get the first-place trophy and she would go home with the second-place trophy. That was why she was running as hard as she could and even diving to get to balls. She wanted to do her very best to win.

But Jeana really was playing well, and she hit two winners in a row to force match point. If Devan didn't get this point, she would be beaten. She tossed the ball up in the air, kept her eyes on it, and hit her serve as hard as she could. It went into the corner of the service square but Jeana was ready. She hit the return really hard. Devan knew she would have to sprint hard to get to the ball. She flew across the court but couldn't get there. She watched the ball hit the court and knew that it was right on the edge of the line. It was just barely in.

For just a second, Devan was tempted to call the ball out. If she did, she would win the point and the match would continue. She might even be able to come back and win. She almost yelled, "Out!" but stopped herself.

She remembered talking to a Sunday school teacher who asked her about playing tennis. Devan was proud to tell her about all the matches she had won. What her teacher said next was something she would never forget:

"I'm so proud of you, Devan. I'm so glad you are a very good tennis player. Winning is a lot of fun and makes us feel great. But you know why I'm even more proud of you?"

Devan had shaken her head no.

"I've watched you, Devan, and I know you have a good heart. You are honest and always try to do the right thing. That's what makes me most proud.".

Devan sighed. She was so disappointed to have lost. She was happy for Jeana, but most of all, she remembered a teacher who was proud of her for doing the right thing. This made her feel proud of herself.

LIFE LESSON

We all want to win. Winning is fun. But sometimes we want to win so bad that we are tempted to cheat or be dishonest. This is true in sports, in school, and in all areas of life. Winning is great but doing the right thing is even better.

VERSE TO REMEMBER

Don't tell lies to each other; it was your old life with all its wickedness that did that sort of thing; now it is dead and gone. COLOSSIANS 3:9 TLB

TO TALK ABOUT

Has there been a time when you were tempted to tell a lie or cheat? If you have stumbled, have you asked God to forgive you? Why is it best to always do the right thing?

I MADE THE TEAM!

HOW DO YOU TREAT OTHERS WHO AREN'T AS GOOD AS YOU ON THE TEAM?

Eddie dribbled up and down the driveway, first with his left hand and then with his right hand. Each time he got near the garage, he would shoot a jump shot or drive all the way to the basket for a layup.

When his dad pulled up, he hopped out of the car and called out, "Hit me, I'm open!"

Eddie threw his dad a bounce pass and his dad swished a basket from long distance.

"Good shot, Dad," Eddie shouted.

"I think you live on our basketball court," his dad said with a smile. "How's your day been?"

"Dad, you aren't going to believe it," Eddie said excitedly. "I made the team!"

"All right!" his dad said with a huge smile. "I knew you could do it, son."

Eddie was in fifth grade and had been dreaming of the day when he could try out for the school basketball team.

"So are you going to be the star?" his dad asked with a twinkle in his eyes.

"That's why I'm practicing," Eddie answered. "Some of the guys shoot better than me and I'm still not very good dribbling with my left hand."

"That's what practice is for, Eddie," his dad

answered. "But you're on the team and that's a good start. This is about a perfect day for you."

He was surprised when Eddie frowned.

"What's wrong, son?"

"Jason didn't make the team. He feels really bad. He wouldn't even come over and shoot baskets with me. I really wanted both of us to make the team."

"Oh, that's too bad," Dad answered. "But that doesn't mean you two won't still be best friends."

"I know," Eddie answered. "I just feel bad for him. He doesn't have a dad like you who helps him get better."

Jason lived alone with his mom. She loved him very much and he was a happy kid, but he had told Eddie many times how lucky he was to have a dad who played sports with him.

Eddie and his dad went inside to eat dinner. Both were quiet as they thought about Jason.

"Is everything okay with you two?" Mom asked them.

"I was just thinking," Eddie's dad said. "I want to go outside and play basketball with Eddie."

Eddie looked up with a smile on his face.

"Eddie has homework and he's been outside long enough," Mom said sternly.

That put a frown on Eddie's face.

"But Eddie made the team," his dad said. "And plus, I know he wants to call Jason and see if he will come over and play with us. After all, we have to get Jason ready to make the team next year, don't we, Eddie?"

"We do!" Eddie yelled.

"Use your inside voice," Mom said with raised eyebrows. "But you two go on outside if you want."

"I just have to call Jason first," Eddie said, beaming. "You'll really help him, too, Dad?"

"That's what friends are for, son."

LIFE LESSON

It's great to make the team. But being a great friend means we help others do their very best, too. It's good to celebrate when you do something good in sports, but be sure to help your teammates do their best as well.

VERSE TO REMEMBER

Treat others just as you want to be treated.
LUKE 6:31 CEV

TO TALK ABOUT

Who is a friend that you can help do their very best at school or in sports?

RED CARD!

HAVE YOU EVER LET YOURSELF GET SO ANGRY THAT YOU HATE SOMEONE?

Everywhere Barry ran on the soccer field, Todd, a kid on the other team, followed him.

Barry had been having a good season with his U12 team. Real good. He had the most goals on his team and had at least one goal every game.

That's why the coach of the other team told Todd, his best player, to shadow Barry wherever he ran.

Every time Barry got the ball, he tried to get away from Todd with a move. He tried a series of crossover steps. He tried the lunge. He tried the helicopter. But no matter what move Barry tried, he could not get past Todd.

As the game went on Barry got more and more frustrated. On one play, he and Todd were both running hard for the ball. They bumped into each other and Barry went sprawling. He jumped up quickly, sure that the referee was going to call a foul on Todd. But the referee didn't think the collision was a foul.

This got Barry even madder. He was steaming. But then it got worse.

Todd stole the ball from him and scored a goal. Now Barry's team was losing by two goals and there wasn't much time left in the game. They were probably going to lose. He was furious that

Todd was getting the better of him.

After Todd scored the goal, as he ran by Barry and said in a loud whisper, "Hey loser, I knew you were no good."

On the next play, after his team kicked off, Barry was so mad he threw an elbow at Todd to get him away from him. This time the referee did call a foul. But not just a foul, he pulled out a red card that meant Barry was kicked out of the game for a dirty play. Barry had never received a yellow card, but now he had a red card and his team had to play with one less player. And they were losing by two goals. He had let his team down.

As he left the field, his coach looked at him sternly and said, "Why would you have done that, Barry? I've never seen you do anything like that."

"I hate that kid," Barry said. "He's dirty and he's a jerk. He was holding and pushing me the whole game and no one called a foul on him."

After the whistle sounded to end the game, Barry's coach called him over.

"I want you to shake hands with the other team like a good sport, but I also want you to apologize for throwing an elbow."

"I can't apologize to Todd," Barry protested. "He's a jerk. He called me a loser."

"Maybe he is and maybe he isn't," Barry's coach responded. "But someone I know is for sure not being a good sport. Even if someone else calls names and acts like a jerk, does that give you permission to be one too?"

The coach's question stung Barry.

"Barry, I know you are a great kid and a great player. No way you are a loser. But today you have let your anger get the best of you. It's okay to get intense. It's even okay to get mad. But it's not okay to do what you did. There's a reason you got a red card."

Barry knew his coach was right. He'd never gotten mad like this before. He realized his anger had caused him to hurt another player, hurt his team, and even hurt himself by letting Todd get under his skin.

Getting in line to shake hands with the other team was tough. It was even tougher to apologize to Todd.

To his surprise, Todd apologized back to him: "Sorry for calling you a name and acting like a jerk. It won't happen again."

"I won't be throwing an elbow at you again," Barry answered. "But I am going to score next time we play!"

Todd laughed and said, "Not if I can help stop you!"

LIFE LESSON

Everyone gets angry. Anger is not a sin. But when we let anger become a habit or hurt others because of our anger, then it is definitely God who wants it out of our lives immediately. When you feel angry, it's time to say a prayer and ask God to help you clear your mind and heart from a destructive attitude.

VERSE TO REMEMBER

When you are angry, don't let that anger make you sin," and don't stay angry all day. EPHESIANS 4:25 ERV

TO TALK ABOUT

Have you ever let yourself get so angry that you have done the wrong thing? How can we stop anger from getting the best of us?

DON'T QUIT FIGHTING!

DO YOU WANT TO QUIT WHEN YOU ARE LOSING OR NOT DOING WELL?

Cody was in his second year of wrestling. It was a hard but fun sport. There was lots of running, lots of stretching, lots of core exercises, and you always had to keep an eye on what you ate so you could make your weight class at weigh-ins before every match. Cody was the strongest he had ever been and was in the best shape of his life. He liked that his arm, chest, and stomach muscles were really popping out. He also really enjoyed his coach and teammates. Coach pushed them hard, but he was also very funny and he cared about him and his teammates.

Unfortunately, Cody found himself in the middle of a match that sure seemed hard and sure wasn't very fun.

As soon as the whistle sounded, the kid he was wrestling against, Alex, made a lightning fast move to snag his ankle and take him down on the mat. hard. *Wow, that was fast,* was all Cody had time to think before he was falling toward the mat. He immediately twisted around and got on all fours to attempt a sit-out move to escape from Alex's hold on him. But every time he was able to push his body up off the mat, Alex got a new hold on his wrist or his elbow and drove him back down. Alex was moving quickly to try to put a half nelson on Cody so he could flip him onto his back and pin him.

With Alex on top of him the whole first period, Cody was already feeling a lot of fatigue. He started the second period in the down position. It was more of the same. Alex couldn't flip him over to pin him, but Cody could escape from Alex's holds. When the third period began, Alex shot forward like a rocket and escaped from Cody's hold. Cody groaned inside. This was not going well. Then Alex tried the very same take-down move that he used to start the match. It worked again.

Cody had never been pinned before, but he wasn't very confident he could fight Alex off for the whole third period. He had to hang on for only ninety seconds, but every second felt like an hour.

"Keep fighting, Cody!" his coach yelled. "Get up on your knees."

"Keep wrestling!" his dad called out.

"Cody! Cody! Cody! Cody!" a couple of his friends were chanting in unison.

Cody's arms felt like wet noodles. He was gasping for air. Every part of his body wanted to just quit. But in a final push, he did get himself up on all fours. Then, using the last of his energy, Cody finally got his sit-out move to work. He got a reverse and was on top of Alex. The sudden change took Alex by surprise and he made a big mistake. He reached his arm back. Cody leaped forward and caught Alex in a hold that flipped Alex onto his back. For the next thirty seconds he squeezed as hard as he could to keep Alex on his back and not let him escape. Cody couldn't believe it when the ref slapped his hand on the mat and shouted, "Pin!"

After thinking he had lost, Cody had kept fighting and won the match.

After shaking hands with Alex, the referee held his arm up to show he had won. Cody was so tired he could barely smile. He looked over at Alex and Alex said, "Good job. That was a great move. How did you do it?"

Now Cody did smile as he said, "I was lucky to beat you. I have no idea how I did it. I just kept fighting."

LIFE LESSON

When life gets tough at school or with a friend or in your sport, the natural response is to want to quit. But even if you lose a match, you'll always be a winner if you never quit. Sometimes you just have to keep fighting!

VERSE TO REMEMBER

My brothers and sisters, you will face all kinds of trouble. When you do, think of it as pure joy. Your faith will be tested. You know that when this happens it will produce in you the strength to continue. JAMES 1:2-3 NIRV

TO TALK ABOUT

Have you ever had a time when you just wanted to quit? What did you do? How can you keep doing your best even when it is hard?

A PAINFUL TUMBLE

HOW DO YOU HANDLE GETTING HURT IN A GAME?

Jennifer was excited all week about Saturday morning. Her gymnastics team had been working hard for months, and they would be doing an exhibit for their parents to show all they had learned. This was also the day they would be practicing for their first meet that was only weeks away.

Jennifer was best at floor exercises. She wasn't very good on the balance beam but had practiced hard and could do the entire routine without falling. She was proud to show her parents what she could do now.

On Saturday morning, Jennifer's mom woke her up early for breakfast.

"I'm too nervous to eat," Jennifer said.

"You'll do better if you eat." Her mom laughed. "You need your energy."

Jennifer munched her favorite cereal but barely tasted it. She was too excited about the exhibit. She ran upstairs to get changed into her uniform. When she came back downstairs, her mom fixed her hair in pigtails with the bows she liked.

Once the exhibit began, Jennifer focused on doing everything perfectly. The team started with a dance and tumbling routine that the parents loved. There was lots of cheering and clapping.

Next was the vaults. Everything went perfectly. Jennifer was a little nervous when it was time to do the balance beam. She knew other girls would do better, but she was proud of how she had worked to do well. Her coach helped her up and she began the routine.

Jennifer wasn't sure how it happened, but when she went from a handstand to her feet, she completely lost balance and fell. All she knew was that she was in the worst pain of her life. When she looked down at her ankle, to her dismay, she could see that it was already swelling up.

Her coach and parents ran over to her. She cried as her coaches, parents, and teammates gathered around her to see how bad her injury was. Her dad picked her up in his arms and carried her to the car. The drove to the emergency room of the closest hospital. After waiting for what seemed like forever as her parents filled out paperwork, the doctor finally was ready to see her.

"I don't think it's broken, but we better get an X-ray," the doctor said.

That meant waiting even longer. She cried on her mom's shoulder while they waited for the results. A little later, the doctor returned.

"The good news is your ankle isn't broken," she said to Jennifer. "The bad news is you have a bad sprain."

"Does that mean I can still can go to the meet in a couple weeks?" Jennifer asked.

"I'm afraid that probably won't be possible," the kind doctor answered. "You're going to be just fine, but it's going to take at least a couple weeks before you can do any more gymnastics. You're going to have to wear a brace, and for the first week you're going to have to walk with crutches."

Jennifer cried some more. She was so disappointed. This was supposed to be a wonderful morning but it had turned into something awful. Her ankle throbbed.

Her parents tried to cheer her up, but Jennifer felt miserable the rest of the day. She finally fell asleep and took a long nap on the living room couch.

"Are you hungry?" her mom asked when she woke up.

"I guess so," Jennifer answered sadly.

"You do know that everything is going to be good?" her mom asked.

"I guess so," Jennifer said.

"You know that God is with us, even when we are hurting, right?" Mom asked.

Jennifer thought about that question. She realized it was true. She knew other kids who had been on crutches at school. She knew they were just fine. She knew that some people were hurt all the time. One of the kids in her school had to get around in a wheelchair.

For the first time since that morning, Jennifer smiled. Then she grimaced when she tried to put weight on her foot. Then she smiled again.

"Mom, thanks for reminding that God is with me even when I hurt."

LIFE LESSON

It doesn't just happen in sports. In life, we slip or bump into something or get sick, and all of a sudden everything seems to hurt. God reminds us that He is with us in good times and tough times. If we trust Him, everything works out and we can live with happiness and joy.

VERSE TO REMEMBER

God is our protection and source of strength. He is always ready to help us in times of trouble.
PSALM 46:1 ERV

TO TALK ABOUT

Think of a time when you got hurt in sports or just in everyday activities. How did that make you feel? Did you learn any lessons about overcoming tough times?

I DON'T LIKE THAT KID

WHAT DO YOU DO WHEN A TEAMMATE DOESN'T LIKE YOU—AND YOU DON'T LIKE THEM?

Robert was practicing free throws after practice. For some reason he had been missing a lot of free throws lately. He shot the ball toward the basket. It clunked off the front of the rim.

"You couldn't throw a ball in the ocean!" Joey, one of his teammates, yelled at him. "You are the worst shoot I've ever seen."

Robert ignored him and shot again. This time it clunked off the back of the room. Joey started laughing out loud and pointing at Robert. Then he acted like he was shooting a basket and fell down.

"Hey look everybody," yelled Joey. "I can't make a basket."

He was having a lot of fun making fun of Robert. Robert wondered why Joey always treated him so badly. They had never gotten along because Joey was always mean to him. Way back in kindergarten they had even gotten into a fist fight. The boys were taken to the principal's office and were in big trouble. But even after getting a lecture from their principal and their parents, the boys still never got along.

Robert blamed Joey. He minded his own

business and left Joey alone. But Joey always had a put-down ready to throw at Robert. Most of the time he could ignore it, but times like this, he really wanted to teach Joey a lesson. Robert knew it wasn't right to get in fights, but sometimes he just wanted to punch Joey in the nose.

"Let's see you miss another shot!" Joey yelled. "Bet you can't make it!"

What should he do? He was so sick and tired of Joey giving him a hard time. One of his friends, Gary, walked in and waved to Robert. Robert waved back. When Gary got over to where Robert was standing, he asked, "Is Joey giving you a bad a time again?"

"You better believe it," Robert answered, shaking his head.

"You know why he does it, don't you?" Gary asked.

"Of course I do," Robert answered. "Because he hates me."

"Well, that's only part of the reason," Gary said. "He doesn't like you because he knows you don't like him."

"What?!" Robert protested. "When have I ever been mean to him?"

"Well, you're not mean to him, but it's obvious you don't like him because you always do your very best to ignore him."

"Is it that obvious?" Robert asked.

"Very obvious!" Gary said.

That night before bed, Robert started thinking

about Joey and what Robert had said. Was it possible that he shared some of the blame for why the two boys didn't get along? *If I tried to be nice to him, could Joey and I actually be friends?* he wondered.

Robert didn't know the answer, but as he said a short prayer, he asked God to give him the desire and strength to give it a try.

LIFE LESSON

It is almost impossible to get along with everyone. We just don't connect with everybody the same way. It is easy to be friends with some people and hard to be friends with others. But we should always try our best to treat everyone the same way we want to be treated. We should do our best to get along with others.

VERSE TO REMEMBER

Do all that you can to live in peace with everyone. ROMANS 12:18 NLT

TO TALK ABOUT

Who is someone you have a hard time being friends with? What can you do to be a peacemaker?

THE GREEN-EYED MONSTER

WE WILL ALL FEEL JEALOUS TOWARD OTHERS SOMETIMES, BUT HOW WILL YOU SLAY THE GREEN-EYED MONSTER?

"Honey, what do you mean you don't want to invite Sabrina to your birthday party" Jessica's mom asked in surprise. "You and Sabrina have been best friends since you both started walking."

"I just don't want her there," Jessica said.

"Have you two had a fight?" her mom asked.

"Not really," Jessica answered.

"Then why aren't you inviting her for your sleepover?"

"It's hard to explain," Jessica said.

But Jessica knew what was on her mind. She was tired of being around Sabrina because Sabrina was so good at everything she did. Definitely better than Jessica. She was prettier. She was more popular. She got better grades. Now she was a better swimmer than her. It used to be that swimming was the only thing Jessica was better at than Sabrina. But not anymore. At their swim meet the previous weekend, Jessica did okay. She got third place in the backstroke and the breaststroke. But Sabrina took first in three events. Three gold medals at one meet. She was given another medal for being the outstanding swimmer of the entire meet.

It wasn't that Sabrina bragged about anything. She really didn't seem to care that much about winning or losing. She just always won. She was actually nice to everyone, but she and Jessica were next-door neighbors and had always been best friends.

"Well, are you going to try?" Jessica's mom asked her.

"Try what?" Jessica said.

"You said it's difficult to explain why you don't want Sabrina at your party. Are you at least going to try and explain?"

"Mom, I don't want to talk about it."

"But I do," her mother said.

"Okay, I'll just say it then," Jessica mumbled in embarrassment. "I'm jealous of her. I'm tired of Sabrina being the best at everything."

She was expecting her mother to give her a lecture or scold her, so Jessica was surprised when her mother said, "I don't think you have anything to be jealous of, but I understand how you feel."

"How can you know how I feel?" Jessica asked, curious.

"Because when I was a little bit older than you, I had something similar happen to me."

For the next twenty minutes, Jessica's mom told her how jealous she had felt toward a cousin. They, too, had been best friends. She still felt horrible that she had said some very harsh things to her cousin and damaged the relationship for years. Later they made up, but her mom was sad that she had lost a wonderful friend for years.

"I never knew about that," Jessica said. "I didn't know you ever had problems like that."

Her mom laughed and said, "Jessica, honey, everyone has problems like that. We all face temptation, including the temptation to let jealousy ruin a wonderful friendship. I hope you'll think about not inviting Sabrina and change your mind."

With a tear in the corner of her eye, Jessica said, "I don't have to think about it, Mom. I want Sabrina to be at my sleepover."

LIFE LESSON

Sometimes jealousy sneaks into our hearts like a thief in the night; sometimes jealousy roars into our hearts like a hungry lion. Jealousy makes us feel bad about who we are and take it out on someone else. It makes us compare ourselves to others. It keeps us from feeling good about our own success and the success of others. The best way to get rid of jealousy is to remember how much God loves you.

VERSE TO REMEMBER

Love is patient and kind. Love is not jealous, it does not brag, and it is not proud. I CORINTHIANS 13:4 ERV

TO TALK ABOUT

Have you ever let jealousy hurt a relationship with a friend? What will you do to get rid of jealousy the next time it sneaks up on you?

PICKING DAISIES

WHAT DO YOU DO TO HELP A TEAMMATE WHO ISN'T DOING VERY WELL?

"Torrie! Torrie! The ball is coming!"

The soccer coach usually didn't yell at his girls, but Torrie had been having a hard time paying attention this game. Her mind seemed to be a million miles away. She kept looking over at the horses in a pasture next to the soccer fields. When she wasn't looking at the horses, she was looking at the ground and kicking at dirt.

At halftime, the coach had said to Torrie, "We are playing soccer and all you want to do is pick daisies!"

She wasn't really picking daisies. And he wasn't really mad at her. He just wanted her to pay attention to the game and help the team win.

Torrie liked soccer a lot. But sometimes her mind wandered. It happened to her at school, too. The teacher would be talking about math, but her mind would be on a story the class read earlier.

The coach called for Torrie to get her head up and see the ball that was rolling in her direction, but it was too late. A girl on the other team got there first, whizzed by Torrie, and scored a goal.

Morgan was Torrie's best friend. Morgan didn't have any problem focusing on the game. She was always first to the ball. When Morgan saw

Torrie give up an easy goal, she was mad. She was ready to yell at Torrie and let her know she was hurting the team.

Right before some mean words came out of Morgan's mouth, she stopped. Torrie really was a nice person. She was just an okay soccer player, but she did many other things that made her laugh and be happy.

As Morgan trotted over to Torrie, she could see that her friend felt terrible. She might even be ready to cry. Instead of yelling at her, Morgan gave her a pat on the back and said, "Come on, Torrie, get your head up and start playing harder. Don't quit now just because you had a bad play. You can do it."

Those words of encouragement were just what Torrie needed to hear. She was finally able to focus and pay attention to the game.

With the score tied, a player on the other team was pushing the ball down the field. This time, the coach didn't need to yell for Torrie's attention to tell her the ball was coming. Torrie was ready. When the ball came loose, she was a step ahead of the other girl and kicked it safely to Morgan, who was close to the sideline. Morgan immediately kicked the ball ahead to another player on their team, Holly, who was able to dribble forward and score a goal. Their team had won.

Morgan listened as the coach and parents and other spectators cheered and yelled, "Way to go, Holly! Great goal, Holly!"

Morgan ran up and gave Holly a hug, too, saying, "Great goal!"

But she quickly ran back to her friend and said, "Great job, Torrie! You set up the winning score. Great job!"

Torrie smiled and said, "Thanks for the encouragement, Morgan. If you hadn't told me I could do it, I might still be picking daisies!"

LIFE LESSON

Everyone has a bad game. Everyone makes mistakes. Everyone has a day when their mind is somewhere else and they don't do their best to help a team win. Instead of getting mad and yelling at teammates, be an encourager who helps them do their very best. You will help them *and* your team!

VERSE TO REMEMBER

So encourage one another with the hope you have. Build each other up. In fact, that's what you are doing. I THESSALONIANS 5:11 NIRV

TO TALK ABOUT

Has there been a time when you didn't have your best game and someone yelled at you? Has there been a time when someone encouraged you?

WORDS MATTER

WHAT DO YOU DO IF SOMEONE ON YOUR TEAM CONSTANTLY USES FOUL LANGUAGE?

Kenny couldn't believe what he was hearing. Sure, he had heard other kids use cuss words plenty of times at school, but never like this. It was his first year playing football and he wasn't expecting this. Part of the problem was there were so many guys on the team and the field was so big, coaches couldn't keep up with everything being done or said. The head coach was a friend of his parents and he didn't believe the coach would allow that kind of language.

He was in line for a tackling drill, but his mind was on what was being said behind him. He wondered to himself, *Should I say something to coach?* If he did and the other kids found out, what would they think of him? Would they lose respect for him because he was a tattler?

Then he wondered if he should say something to the guy behind him in line. He had only known Mark for a couple days. But Kenny definitely knew that Mark used the worst language of anyone on the team. Before he could decide whether to say something to Mark and what he might say, he was in the front of the line. It was his turn to tackle the runner. Two orange cones were set up. His job was to stop the runner from getting through.

He looked over. The kid was pretty big. He would have to concentrate.

"Okay, Kenny, knees bent, shoulder pads square, eyes up, and put your helmet on the ball!" his coach yelled before blowing the whistle to tell them to start moving.

Maybe he was a little angry at what he was hearing, but Kenny did keep his eyes up and made a great tackle between the cones. He stopped the runner in his tracks. The loud popping noise brought cheers from his teammates.

"Good, clean tackle, Kenny! Nicely done," his coach called out.

As he trotted to the back of the running back line, several of his teammates thumped his shoulder pads in appreciation for his good form tackle.

"Nice hit, Kenny!" one of his friends yelled.

Kenny continued to think about the bad language he was hearing, particularly from Mark. *When you do things the right way, it has a positive influence on others,* he thought to himself. In the same way, Mark was being a bad influence on others.

Mark went through the same drill and made a pretty good tackle, but the running back dragged him a few extra yards.

"You got to keep your eyes up, Mark!" the coach yelled.

When Mark got to the back of the line, he was muttering some very bad names to describe the coach. That settled it for Kenny. He had to say something.

His heart was pounding as he said, "Mark, I like you as a teammate, but I really don't like the way you are cussing and swearing all the time. I'd really appreciate it if you'd watch your language."

Mark looked at him in astonishment.

"Everyone cusses," he said to Kenny.

"I don't," Kenny answered, "and there's a lot of other guys who don't."

"This is football," Mark said. "You can't be afraid of hearing bad words."

"I'm not afraid," Kenny said. "I just don't think it's right and I don't like it. I'm not the only one. And besides, bad words aren't what make you tough. Good tackling is what makes you a good player."

Mark laughed. Kenny thought he was going to make fun of him. Then to his surprise, Mark said, "You are a good tackler, Kenny. So maybe I need to watch what I say around you."

Kenny wasn't sure if Mark was giving him a hard time or meant what he said. But by the time practice was over, he noticed that Mark hadn't sworn or cussed another time. At least not around him.

LIFE LESSON

Our words matter. We should be positive with what we say. When we start swearing and cussing, it has a negative influence on others—and on ourselves. Your words need to honor God, others, and yourself.

VERSE TO REMEMBER

But now here are the kinds of things you must also get rid of. You must get rid of anger, rage, hate and lies. Let no dirty words come out of your mouths. COLOSSIANS 3:8 NIRV

TO TALK ABOUT

Are you ever tempted to use bad language? Have you or friends you know gotten in the bad habit of swearing and cussing? What is the best way to break a bad habit?

STAY POSITIVE

WHAT DO YOU DO WHEN YOUR TEAM ISN'T DOING VERY WELL AND YOU KEEP LOSING GAMES?

Could it be? Were they finally going to win a game? Was their losing streak about to end?

Grace's heart was racing. Only ten seconds were left in their basketball game. Their best player, Ellison, had come down with mono at the beginning of the season and had missed all their games. Grace and her teammates still didn't expect to lose nine straight games. They'd been beaten badly in some of the games, but other games were close. They just couldn't hit a shot to finally get a win.

Now their best shooter, Angie, was on the free throw line. They were losing by only one point. If Angie could make one basket, they would probably go into overtime—unless the other team got lucky on a long shot. If Angie could make both baskets, the team would almost for sure get their first win.

"Come on, Angie, you can do it," Grace said over and over in her mind.

Angie eyed the basket. She bent her knees slightly. She lofted up a shot with perfect form.

It's going in, Grace thought, ready to shout for joy. But the orange ball circled around the rim once, hung on the edge for what seemed like an

49

eternity, and rolled outside the goal.

It took all of Grace's discipline not to groan out loud.

The referee handed the ball back to Angie. *This one is going in for sure,* Grace thought. She still put her hands up and tensed up her body to try for a rebound just in case it didn't.

Angie looked calm and confident. She bounced the ball once, twice, three times, just like she always did. Her eyes narrowed as she focused on the basket. Once again, she bent her knees and sent the ball upward with a flick of her wrist.

Go in, go in, go in! Grace thought.

The ball arced toward the basket...it was straight on...but it clunked off the front of the rim. Grace went for the rebound as hard as she could, but even before she heard the whistle, she knew she was going to be called for a fall. She had crashed into another girl's back.

She walked dejectedly down the court, knowing the game was probably lost. And sure enough, the girl she fouled sank both free throws for a three-point lead. Grace took the ball out of bounds, threw it as hard as she could to a teammate at half court, but it bounced off her hands and went out of bounds.

A few agonizing seconds later, the buzzer sounded, and the game was over. Ten straight losses.

After shaking hands to congratulate the other team, Grace and her team huddled up around the coach. All Grace could do was look at the floor.

How can you lose ten straight games? You've got to get lucky at least a few times. They had worked hard but just couldn't grab a victory.

She glanced to her left and right. Everyone else was looking down, too. She looked across the huddle at Angie. Angie looked like she wanted to cry.

"Okay, girls, I want all eyes up," the coach said. "Let's go! Everyone look at me."

Grace looked up.

"I know this year isn't going very well for us as a team," the coach said. "But here's what I want you to know. I appreciate how hard you work. I know each and every one of you are hustling. We're going to win a game before this season is over. Right?"

No one said anything.

"Right?!"

They weren't very loud, but the whole team answered back to the coach, "Yes!"

"I'll tell you how we are going to win," the coach continued.

Now Grace looked at her more intently.

"We are going to stay positive. Every one of us. We are going to stay positive because your attitude makes a difference."

Grace still felt bad about the loss but decided her coach was right. Staying positive gave her team a much better chance of notching a victory.

LIFE LESSON

It's easy to be positive when you are winning all your games. It's much tougher to stay positive when things just don't go right. That's true in sports and it's true in all life. But just as a positive attitude gives you a better chance to win a basketball game, it makes you a winner in every area of your life!

VERSE TO REMEMBER

Christ is the one who gives me the strength I need to do whatever I must do. PHILIPPIANS 4:13 ERV

TO TALK ABOUT

Have you ever gotten discouraged and negative because of the way things are going on your team or in another area of life? What is the best way to turn a bad attitude into a positive attitude?

TOO TALL?

HAVE YOU EVER WISHED YOU WERE A DIFFERENT PERSON?

"Great spike, Kat!" Regina said.

Kat was the star of her volleyball team. Only in sixth grade, she was taller than most boys at her middle school. Not only that, she was almost as tall as her dad now. It felt strange to look at her dad eye-to-eye. He had always seemed so big and tall when she was a little girl.

That was the problem Kat was feeling now. Sure, it was great being tall on the volleyball court. It was a big advantage for her and her team. No one could block her shots. Her coach had even talked to her parents about moving her up a couple of grades to play on the junior varsity team at the high school.

But sometimes being the tallest girl in school made Kat feel awkward.

"Honey, you're beautiful and perfect," her mother would say to her. "You're exactly the way God created you to be."

She knew her mother was right, but Kat still felt embarrassed by her height sometimes. Regina was the setter on her team. She was a great athlete and a great player. And she was perfectly normal in height. Sometimes Kat wished she could look like Regina.

"One more point, let's get it!" Regina yelled.

Kat focused on the action. They had already won two games and only needed one more point to win the match. Another teammate, Krissy, served the ball over the net. The other team easily handled it. The setter placed a perfect pass to the other team's best player. She jumped up to smash the ball, but Kat jumped at the same time and blocked the shot for the point. Her team had won again.

The girls jumped up and down and hugged in the middle of the court before making a line to shake hands with the other team. As she slapped hands with the girls in line, she and the girl whose shot she blocked to win the game were face to face.

"Great game," she said to Kat. "You're just too tall for me."

She said it nicely and Kat knew she wasn't trying to put her down or make her feel bad about herself, but she still felt a pang in her heart. *Why do I have to be so different than everyone else? Why can't I be more normal? Why do I have to be a head taller than all of my friends?*

As they headed toward the locker room, Regina came up next to her.

"What are you frowning about?" she asked.

"I didn't know I was frowning," Kat said.

"Well you are," Regina said. "You look like we just lost the game. Come on, big sister, look like you're happy," she added with a friendly laugh.

"That's the problem," Kat said. "I'm tired of being the big sister. Sometimes I wish I could be five inches shorter so I could be like everyone else."

"Are you crazy?" Regina nearly shouted. "I'd give anything to grow five inches. If you can figure out how to get rid of them, be sure to give them to me!"

Both girls laughed.

"Seriously," Regina said, "you are the most normal person in the world that I know, even if you are a little taller than the rest of us. That only makes us envy you more?"

"Envy?" Kat asked incredulously.

"You better believe we're jealous," Regina said. "I'd give anything to spike a volleyball like you do."

The two girls continued into the locker room where their teammates were laughing and yelling, happy to have won the match. When they saw Kat come in, they started chanting, "Kat! Kat! Kat!"

Maybe I am exactly what God wants me to be, Kat thought.

LIFE LESSON

Too short? Too tall? Too thin? Too thick? Not as gifted as others? A little jealous of how well others do in sports or different areas of life? The answer to all those questions is that you are perfect the way you are. After all, God designed you and He has a special plan for your life. Don't try to be somebody else. Be the best you you can be!

VERSE TO REMEMBER

I praise you, for I am fearfully and wonderfully made. Wonderful are your works; my soul knows it very well. PSALM 139:14 ESV

TO TALK ABOUT

Have you ever wished you were more like someone else? When was the last time you thanked God for making you wonderfully well?

KEEP IMPROVING

ARE YOU WILLING TO WORK HARD TO BE THE BEST PLAYER YOU CAN BE?

Zach looked up at the bright, glaring sun. It really was a hot day. Most of his friends were already at the swimming pool, jumping off the high dive, playing sharks and minnows, eating snow cones, and having towel fights.

He was still on the tennis court, all by himself, practicing his serve. The local YMCA was holding a tennis camp this summer. It started at nine in the morning and was over by eleven. But from the very first time he held a racquet, Zach knew this was a sport he wanted to be good at. So even after all the kids left, he stayed behind. Sometimes the instructor would rally with him for thirty extra minutes. But Zach wanted to get even better. So he begged the instructor to leave a bucket of balls so he could practice his serve.

"You're going to be a great tennis player," the instructor told him. "I think you have a bright future. You'll be good enough to make your team when you get to high school. And who knows, maybe you'll even get to play in college. You just have to keep working at it."

Zach didn't mind working at it. In fact, the only real problem was finding enough other kids his age to practice against.

Still, on this hot summer day, he wondered

if he was crazy not to be at the pool already. He thought about quitting, but then he saw another kid ride up on a bike. He had a backpack with two tennis racquets poking out the top.

Zach had to make a decision. The pool or play some more tennis?

"You want to hit some?" the kid called out.

"You bet," Zach said. "What's your name?"

"Andy, what's yours?"

With introductions finished, Zach and Andy started playing. For the next two hours the boys ran and hit and grunted and sweated. The only times they stopped were to gulp down water. Andy was the best player Zach had ever hit against. He felt like his reflexes and strokes had gotten better in the short time they'd been playing.

Finally, during a break, Andy looked at his phone and said, "I have to head home now. I told my mom I'd be back by two. Do you want to play again at the same time tomorrow?"

Zach thought about the pool. It would feel so good to jump into the cold water and cool off. By playing this long, he would barely have time to get wet. Then he thought about how much fun it was to get better at tennis.

"I'd love to play again tomorrow," Zach said. "See you at noon?"

"I'll be here and ready to go," Andy answered with a smile.

Yep, the pool is great, Zach thought. *But sometimes practicing a little bit longer and working a little bit harder is even funner!*

LIFE LESSON

We all need to have time to play and relax. God doesn't want us to work all the time. But to get really good in our sport or other areas of life, we do need to invest extra time and effort. Giving extra is the key to getting better. Even Jesus, as a young boy, worked hard to grow mentally and physically and spiritually.

VERSE TO REMEMBER

As Jesus grew taller, he continued to grow in wisdom. God was pleased with him and so were the people who knew him. LUKE 2:52 ERV

TO TALK ABOUT

Do you want to get better at your sport? Is there another area of your life where you want to improve? What will it take for you to get better?

THE MISSING BOARD

EVEN WHEN SOMEONE HURTS US, GOD WANTS US TO SHOW FORGIVENESS

Josh couldn't believe it. He was planning to spend the day at a skate park with his brand-new Plan B skateboard. But it wasn't where he left it in the garage. He moved things around and looked high and low but it was nowhere to be found.

He walked around the house to see if he had left it outside. No sign of it. He went inside the house and headed up for his room. He was sure he hadn't brought it up there but he looked anyway. It was nowhere to be found.

He pulled out his phone and called his mom. She had to work until noon this particular Saturday. She picked up on the first ring.

"What do you need, Josh?" she asked. "I have to be quick because I'm working."

"Hey Mom, did you put my new skateboard anywhere?"

"No," she answered. "Why?"

"I can't find it anywhere."

"Did you check the garage?" she asked.

"That's the first place I looked."

"Well, check again, Josh. I'm sure it's hidden behind something."

Josh got off the phone and started searching

for his prized possession again. He had saved up all his birthday and Christmas money from his grandparents to buy what he thought was the best board on the market. Money was always tight at his house, so this was a big deal. Josh had been skating for three years now and attended camp every summer. He had gotten good enough to enter competitions and win some medals. He hoped that one of the skateboard companies would sponsor him with free gear if he kept working at it. His mom never pushed him to be a skater, but she was supportive because he liked it so much. Josh would hate to see the worry on her face if she knew he had lost his board.

He went through the garage, the house, and the yard one more time. The Plan B was gone. He was sick to his stomach but grabbed his old board and started pushing his way to the skate park that was about a mile from his house. Halfway there he ran into a friend, Derrick.

"Josh, I can't believe you let Ben use your new board," was the first thing that came out of Derrick's mouth. "Josh, he busted it up pretty good. Your board is cracked."

Now Josh was really sick to his stomach. He never told Ben he could use his board. That meant that Ben had come by his house, opened the garage door, and just taken it. He had stolen from him.

He said good-bye to Derrick and kept rolling toward the park. The first person he saw was Ben. Ben's face froze when he saw Josh.

"Josh, I'm sorry. I borrowed your new board. I just wanted to test it for myself. I didn't think you'd mind. I messed up bad."

Josh's hands balled up into fists. He wanted to punch Ben in the nose. He remembered what his mom told him about forgiveness and took a deep breath. Better to keep his mouth shut. He and Ben would work out a way for Ben to pay him back for the damage he had done. But he wasn't going to lose a friendship over a broken board.

LIFE LESSON

Forgiving others is one of the ways we show God's love to the world. Forgiving others doesn't mean they aren't responsible for the ways they have hurt us. But it does mean we won't let bitterness and hatred take root in our hearts. Since God forgave us for our sins, we need to be ready to forgive others.

VERSE TO REMEMBER

Don't be angry with each other, but forgive each other. If you feel someone has wronged you, forgive them. Forgive others because the Lord forgave you. COLOSSIANS 3:13 ERV

TO TALK ABOUT

If you were Josh, how would you handle what Ben did? Would you be able to forgive if you knew the person was truly sorry for what they did?

FLYING SO HIGH

HOW DO YOU RESPOND WHEN SOMEONE MAKES FUN OF SOMETHING YOU WORK VERY HARD AT DOING?

Bailey couldn't remember how old she was when she started doing gymnastics. There was a picture in her room that made it look like she was three or four years old. She kept forgetting to ask her mom about it.

She loved gymnastics but she liked other sports too. She played soccer and basketball for a couple years. She wasn't very good at tennis, but she gave that a try too. She went to a volleyball camp because a friend was going. She played in a league for two seasons. But Bailey didn't keep playing the traditional sports because she got into competitive cheerleading. It took a lot of work and time. The team she was on practiced for hours to prepare routines that included stunts, jumps, and tumbling. It was a little bit like gymnastics, but everyone had to work in perfect harmony. If one teammate's timing was off, everything would look wrong and someone might even get hurt. A couple times each year the team would load into vans and go to competitions in great locations. They would be scored by judges based on how hard their routines were and how well they executed them.

It was a lot of hard work and there was a lot

of pressure at the competitions, which were held in large arenas that hosted NBA games and huge concerts.

That's why it hurt her feelings so much when her older brother, Tevin, would see her come home from practice and say things like: "Cheerleading isn't a real sport; anyone can do cheerleading. All you have to do is smile a lot and yell loud and jump around a little."

Bailey would start arguing with Tevin but that only made him tease her more. That would only make her feel worse. She wished there was some way she could convince him that what she did was just as hard, maybe harder, than any other sport.

"He's just teasing you," her mom would say. "Don't worry about it."

Then she would tell Tevin to stop teasing her. But then Tevin teased her for being a crybaby and a tattletale.

A week before a national competition in Orlando, Bailey's cheer coach organized an exhibit. The girls were encouraged to invite friends and family to see them practice their routine one more time before taking the long drive down to Florida.

Bailey's parents made Tevin come along. Since he didn't have baseball practice, he couldn't come up with any excuse not to go. He had never seen the routines Bailey and her team did.

As they went through the final exercise, it was Bailey's job to do very hard moves as one of the flyers. They would do two dismounts. First she had to do a full layout twist and then a pop up tuck. The pop up tuck made her a little nervous because of how high she was thrown up in the air before being caught by her teammates. But it went perfectly and Bailey knew she nailed it.

On the drive home, to her amazement, Tevin almost gave her credit for being a good athlete. He said, "I'm still not sure cheerleading is a sport, but you were incredible, little sis. I never knew you could fly so high."

That made Bailey feel like she was flying inside!

LIFE LESSON

Sometimes friends and even family members will tease us about the things we do or don't do. Most of the time teasing is not meant to hurt our feelings. But sometimes we just don't want to be teased and it really does wound us inside. One way to get people to stop teasing is to ignore them. Another way is to "get back at them" with kindness. What never works is to get mad and start yelling things back at them.

VERSE TO REMEMBER

Don't pay back evil with evil. Don't pay back unkind words with unkind words. Instead, pay back evil with kind words. This is what you have been chosen to do. You will receive a blessing by doing this. I PETER 3:9 NIRV

TO TALK ABOUT

Do you ever get carried away with "trash talk" or teasing a friend? How do you know when it's time to stop teasing and start being an encourager?

ARE YOU READY?

ARE YOU PREPARED WHEN IT'S GAME TIME?

David was all fired up for baseball season. He and one of his neighbors, Kevin, had been playing catch and hitting balls to each other since the first day the weather warmed up. There were even a few days that were really cold when they went outside to throw the ball around. Kevin didn't mind coming inside with red cheeks and freezing hands because of bad weather. He just wanted to get ready for summer baseball.

On Saturday mornings, David's mom would take the two boys to the batting cage and let them hit baseballs that were pitched from a machine. His family didn't have a lot of money, so David did chores for neighbors to help his mom pay for the time in the cage.

Yes, David was fired up. He got even more enthused when his new team, the Wildcats, started practicing a couple nights each week. The coach was very happy with how both he and Kevin were doing. They were hitting well. They fielded every ground ball, even the ones that took a bad bounce, hardly ever making an error. Both boys were hitting the ball very well.

When the coach handed out new uniforms the practice before their first game, David could barely contain his excitement. They were purple and white with a snarling wildcat on the front. He would have worn his uniform to bed instead of pajamas if his mom hadn't said, "No way!"

The first game of the season, the Wildcats won easily. Kevin played center field and David played first base. He even got to pitch the last inning to earn his first ever save.

After the game, the coach awarded a game ball to the best player of the game. David was surprised and very pleased when the ball was handed to him. He beamed with pride.

On the drive home, David's mom asked him how he had done so well.

"Easy, Mom," he answered.

"Really? It didn't look easy to me when you were throwing strikes right over the plate. And it sure didn't look easy when you hit a double your first time at bat. That actually kind of looked hard to me."

"Mom, when you are prepared, everything is easier," David said with a laugh. "You should know that. You're the one who has told me that about my school work a million times."

David's mom laughed and said, "I didn't know you were listening to every word I said. I am impressed. I don't remember telling you that a million times."

"Well, maybe not a million times," David said, "but you've sure said it a lot."

"Well I'm glad you were listening and I'm proud of you for being so prepared," she said. "So, what was your secret? How did you make yourself work so hard to get so much better this season?"

"I don't," David said. "Kevin and I just did it."

"Well, I think I know your secret, young man," David's mom said.

"Yeah?"

"You put your heart into it. There might be some kids who are bigger or faster or stronger than you, but you give it your all. And that's the secret for doing anything great in life."

"Is this going to be one of those lessons you remind me of a million times?" David asked, pretending to be serious.

"I don't have to remind you with baseball," his mom said, smiling. "But I might have to mention it a few times to help you get your schoolwork done in time!"

LIFE LESSON

Enthusiasm, loving what we do, is the secret for success. When we have passion and enthusiasm, even the hard work of preparation becomes fun!

VERSE TO REMEMBER

In all the work you are given, do the best you can. Work as though you are working for the Lord, not any earthly master. COLOSSIANS 3:23 ERV

TO TALK ABOUT

What are you most enthusiastic about in life? How can you get fired up in life

FACING YOUR GIANTS

DO YOU EVER GET SCARED BEFORE A GAME? HOW DO YOU HANDLE YOUR FEARS?

"They're going to kill us," Tamara said. "They never lose!"

Five girls were in the back of a minivan on their way to an out-of-state soccer tournament. They were looking at the tournament schedule. Tamara pointed out that their first game was against a team from Texas that usually won whatever tournament it played in. Many of the players were from countries where soccer was the favorite sport, so they had grown up dribbling a soccer ball.

"They won last year and there were teams from five different states. We don't have a chance."

"The only reason we get to go is because we win a lot too," said Kendra. "If we weren't good we wouldn't even be invited to play."

"We may be good, but they're great," Tamara said. "I watched them last year. They are unbelievable. They have a forward that scored five goals in one game. No one can take the ball away from her."

"Five goals in one game?" Kendra asked with a whistle. "That's unreal."

Suddenly a voice sounded from the front seat: "Should I turn the van around and take you girls home?"

"What? No!" five voices sounded in unison.

"Well, why should we even go down there if we've already lost?" Kendra's dad asked. "What's the point in playing?"

"Dad, we're just talking," Kendra said.

"I know you're just talking but I'm not sure it's getting you ladies ready to do your best. You all do remember the story of David and Goliath, don't you? I'm not guaranteeing you'll win, but I've seen your team play a lot of games and I know you have a chance against anybody."

"Against the women's US soccer team?" Tamara asked, which got all the girls laughing.

"Okay, maybe you aren't ready to beat our national team, but I know you're ready to do great against any team your age. Now no more talk about losing before the game starts. I'll definitely have to turn the van around."

"Dad!" Kendra said.

"He's just kidding," Tamara said, giving Kendra a nudge with her elbow.

"Well, you're the one who said we're going to get killed," Kendra said.

"Okay, I exaggerated a little. And that girl who scored five goals?"

"What about her?" one of the other girls asked.

"She's not nearly big enough to be a giant, so maybe we can win."

That got all five girls laughing.

Maybe they could win, maybe they would lose, but they were ready to face a giant of a team in the first game of their soccer tournament.

LIFE LESSON

Fear can discourage us and make us want to quit before we even get started. We need to remember that with faith and hope, we can face any giant with confidence. This is true in sports, but it is also true in every area of life.

VERSE TO REMEMBER

I am the Lord your God, who holds your right hand. And I tell you, "Don't be afraid! I will help you." ISAIAH 41:13 ERV

TO TALK ABOUT

Have there been situations where you were so afraid you just wanted to run away? How will God help you face your giants?

I DON'T WANT TO MOVE!

DO YOU BELIEVE GOD WILL BRING PEOPLE INTO YOUR LIFE TO LEND A HELPING HAND?

Leslie still couldn't believe her family had moved. She knew her dad had gotten a big promotion, but she loved everything about where they lived before in North Carolina: she loved their house, her school, her church, her softball team, and especially her friends. It just didn't seem fair to her that they had to move.

After a month, she didn't like anything about their new city. She missed her friends. Her dad came home from work and said he had found a fast-pitch softball league and that there was still time for her to get on a team.

"I don't want to play," Leslie told her dad.

"But you love softball," he said to her.

"That was because I had friends on my team," she said angrily. "I don't know anybody here. I don't want to be on a stupid softball team."

"Well, I've already set up a time for you to meet the coach and his daughter, so we're at least going to do that."

"I don't want to meet a new coach. I want to move back to North Carolina and be with my team there."

"Well, we both know that's not going to happen, so we're going to at least go and say hi to the new coach."

Leslie sulked all that day and woke up in a bad mood. She definitely didn't want to join a new team and was mad that her dad was making her meet a new coach. She doubted she would like the coach's daughter either. She buried her head in a book and lay on the couch, reading all day. When her dad got home, she groaned. She didn't want to leave the house.

"Let's go, Leslie," he said.

"I don't want to," she answered.

"I'm not going to make you join a new team, but I am telling you we are going to meet the coach and his daughter. We're going to see them at the Burger Shack."

Leslie did like the food at Burger Shack. She got up slowly and headed for the car. She and her dad didn't talk on the way over. When they walked inside, a man waved a hand and she and her dad headed over to the table.

"This is my daughter Tiffany," the coach, Mr. Brooks, said to Leslie. "She's been looking forward to meeting you."

It wasn't an instant friendship, but it wasn't long before Leslie and Tiffany were talking nonstop. Tiffany had just moved to town a year before and told her how hard it was to feel at home, but now she loved it. Before dinner was over, Leslie let her dad and Mr. Brooks know that she wanted to be on the team.

It didn't take too many practices before Leslie had a friend not only in Tiffany but in every girl on the team. She still missed her friends in North Carolina, but she quickly came to realize that there are nice people anywhere you move. By the time she started school in the fall, her new city felt like home.

"Dad," she said one evening when he arrived home.

"Yes?" he responded.

"I want to thank you for helping me meet friends here. And I'm sorry I was so difficult when we first moved here."

"Anything for my daughter," he said with a smile. "I'm glad I could help."

"Well, if you really mean anything, can you take us all to the Burger Shack for dinner?"

LIFE LESSON

New experiences can be difficult. A new city, a new team, a new school, a new church—anything new can be hard to accept. But when we open our hearts to others, we discover that God has wonderful new friendships and experiences for us.

VERSE TO REMEMBER

"I say this because I know the plans that I have for you." This message is from the Lord. "I have good plans for you. I don't plan to hurt you. I plan to give you hope and a good future." JEREMIAH 29:11 ERV

TO TALK ABOUT

Is it easy or hard for you to meet new friends? When is a time when you were nervous about a new place but met new friends that made it wonderful?

MY MVP!

SOMETIMES THE MOST VALUABLE PLAYER ISN'T THE BEST PLAYER.

My name is Carrie and I want to tell you about someone who changed my life. Her name is Sydney. I met her on the school volleyball team in fourth grade. She is the person who helped me love God, love myself, and love others. She is the best teammate I've ever known. Our team wins a lot of games and I think she is definitely our MVP!

Here's what might surprise you. Sydney isn't a good volleyball player. The truth is she can't play at all. She was born with a rare condition that has kept her in a wheelchair.

But her attitude is unbelievable. She is so wise and so kind. I thought it was crazy when I heard she wanted to be on the volleyball team. I was even more surprised when our coach said yes, she could join the team. I didn't see any way she could help our team. I couldn't have been more wrong.

I was going through a real tough time where I was very unhappy. My parents got divorced and I just hated that. I wanted my family to live together all the time. I didn't like visiting dad one night a week and every other weekend.

It was Sydney that noticed how sad I was. She asked me what was going on. When words started tumbling out of my mouth, she listened. When I started crying, she started crying too. I couldn't believe someone who had enough problems of her own would care enough about my problems to cry with me.

It wasn't just me. She was great with everyone. Always checking to see how we were doing. She would always ask if she could say a prayer for us. Nobody had ever asked me that before.

After one match, I asked Sydney how she was so happy all the time. I asked her if it didn't discourage her to be in a wheelchair all the time.

She said, "I'm happy because I know Jesus loves me and lives in my heart. I know He is always with me and will help me overcome any difficulties. And He can do for you what He did for me."

No surprise, she asked if she could pray for me. But then she asked something different. She asked me if I would like to pray. I didn't go to church back then, but I'd been to places where people prayed, but I don't think I'd ever prayed from my own heart. She helped me with some words to tell God I was sorry for my sins and that I wanted to be a brand-new person on the inside.

I still get discouraged sometimes, but I have to admit, ever since Sydney shared God's love with me, I've been a new person. I read from my Bible and say a prayer every day. I don't know if I'll ever be as wise and kind as Sydney, but I know I'm growing closer to God every day.

"When people ask me who the best player is on my volleyball team, my answer is very easy. It's Sydney, of course. She'll always be my MVP for teaching me how to love God, others, and myself."

LIFE LESSON

There are a lot of things that we care about in life. It's a very good thing to try hard in school and sports and other areas. But nothing is more important than knowing that you are forgiven and that Jesus lives in your heart. That's when you become a new person and learn to love God, others, and yourself.

VERSE TO REMEMBER

For God so loved the world that He gave His only begotten Son, that whoever believes in Him should not perish but have everlasting life. JOHN 3:16 NKJV

TO TALK ABOUT

Do you know that God forgives you? Have you asked Jesus to come into your life? If not, now would be a great time to pray a simple prayer to be saved. If you have already invited Christ into your life, now would be a good time to say a prayer of thanksgiving.

KEEP RUNNING!

ARE YOU WILLING TO KEEP GOING, TO NOT QUIT, WHEN YOUR SPORT GETS TOUGH?

Jake was small for his age. He played football for two years but kept getting hurt. He didn't like it when his dad said he was too small to play football, but he had to admit, his dad was right. He tried out for basketball, but not only was he the shortest guy at tryouts, he was also the worst dribbler. Basketball wasn't for him. He tried baseball but didn't like standing around in right field. Jake was frustrated because he wanted to play on a sports team. But what could he be good at?

What happened the summer before fifth grade was almost an accident. He went over to his school to see if the gym was open. He might not be able to make the basketball team but he thought it would be fun to shoot baskets inside. When he rode his bike up to the side entrance, he saw a group of kids with his PE teacher, Mr. Hollingwood.

"Are you here to join the running club?" Mr. Hollingwood asked Jake.

"Uh, not really," Jake answered. "I was here to shoot some hoops in the gym."

"Well, the gym is closed so you might as well run with us," Mr. Hollingwood said.

"Sure," Jake said.

He rode his bike a lot so he figured he wouldn't have any problems keeping up with the other kids.

"Let me warn you, we're running a 5K today," Mr. Hollingwood said. "Do you think you can handle that?"

"I think so," Jake answered. "How far is that in miles?"

"It's just a tiny bit more than three miles," Mr. Hollingwood answered. "You sure you want to try?"

Jake just nodded and started running with a pack of about twelve other kids from his school. Halfway through the run, some of the other kids were gasping for breath. One boy stopped running.

"We'll be waiting for you," Mr. Hollingwood yelled over his shoulder. He looked over at Jake and said, "He knows the way back to the school. I'll check on him after we're through."

Jake nodded in agreement. Soon it was only Jake and two other kids that were keeping up with Mr. Hollingwood. As they neared the school parking lot, Mr. Hollingwood called out, "Now it's time to kick. Run hard the rest of the way."

To Jake's amazement and Mr. Hollingwood's surprise, Jake was the only one who kept up with the teacher.

"I've got to make sure everyone gets back okay," the teacher said to Jake. "But I expect to see you back here in two days. We run three times a week."

"I think I can," Jake said.

"I hope so," said Mr. Hollingwood. "You're a natural runner and I'm going to need you on the cross-country team this fall."

Jake rode his bike home with a smile on his face the whole way. He'd found the perfect sport for him.

LIFE LESSON

We aren't all good at the same things. Each of us have different gifts. It's that way in the church and it's that way in sports. If you don't succeed at a sport right away, don't feel bad or worry about it. All that means is that you haven't found the right sport for you yet.

VERSE TO REMEMBER

We all have gifts. They differ according to the grace God has given to each of us. ROMANS 12:6 NIRV

TO TALK ABOUT

Have you discovered some things you are really good at? What do you think your gifts are?

BUZZER BEATER

HAVE YOU EVER DREAMED ABOUT SCORING THE WINNING BASKET?

He was supposed to be filling out a math worksheet, but all Brandon could think about was his basketball game after school. He could picture it in his mind and started imagining what might happen.

There's only five seconds to go. The Bobcats are losing by one point. It doesn't look good for the home team. Wait! What just happened? Brandon has stolen the ball. Now he's dribbling it down the court. All five guys for the other team are surrounding him. No way can he score in time. Wait just a minute, folks. Brandon is spinning with the ball. There is only one second left on the clock. He is jumping. The shot is out of his hands. I can't believe it, Brandon has just hit a twenty-foot jump shot to win the game for the Bobcats. Brandon has won the game! Brandon has won the game!

"Brandon!"

Brandon looked up with a start. He had been imagining the perfect ending to a basketball game. His teacher was standing over his desk and looking at him closely.

"Is there a reason everyone else in class has finished the math assignment but you?"

"Uh, I'm just slow today," Brandon said sheepishly.

"Either that or someone named Brandon is daydreaming again. Do you want to tell us what you were thinking about?" she asked.

"Uh, no," Brandon stammered. "I need to hurry up and finish this worksheet."

"If you want to play in your basketball game, you indeed better have this assignment finished," she said to him.

With a gulp, Brandon realized he better get a move on it. He chased his daydreams away and got busy.

The game was played after school in the gym. A lot of students and parents crowded onto the wooden benches to watch the Bobcats play. The game didn't go exactly how Brandon imagined it would, but sure enough, with very few seconds on the clock, the Bobcats were losing by one point and their team had possession of the ball for one last chance to win the game.

This is my chance, Brandon thought. *My dreams can come true. I can shoot a buzzer beater to win the game.*

A teammate passed him the ball and Brandon started dribbling toward the goal as fast as he could. But as he looked up, he realized there were two players from the other team guarding him. That meant two things. First, it was going to be hard to get a shot off. Second, someone else was open. Out of the corner of his eye he spied Michael, who was wide open under the basket. Brandon wanted to shoot the winning shot so bad but knew the smart thing to do was to pass the ball. That's exactly what he did. He bounced a pass to Michael, who scored an easy layup right before the buzzer sounded.

For just a second, Josh was disappointed it wasn't him who had made the basket. But as the crowd went crazy he realized that he had done exactly what he was supposed to do to help his team win. He made sure the right guy took the shot.

LIFE LESSON

In sports, sometimes we get to be the scorer, but sometimes our job is to pass the ball so someone else scores. Either way, we help our team win. In life, sometimes we are in the spotlight, but many more times we will help others shine. Be happy either way!

VERSE TO REMEMBER

None of you should look out just for your own good. Each of you should also look out for the good of others. PHILIPPIANS 2:4 NIRV

TO TALK ABOUT

Who in your life has helped you to be the best you can be? What are ways you can assist others in doing their best?

A FIRST-TEAM ATTITUDE

HOW DO YOU RESPOND IF YOU ARE NOT A STARTER ON YOUR TEAM?

The team was huddled up on the sideline. The game was about to begin. Coach was giving final instructions: "It's going to be a tough game, guys. We're playing a really good team. But we're a really good team too! Now play smart. Stay with your assignment. Pay attention and play hard! Let's hear Eagles on three."

The whole team reached a hand into the circle and shouted together, "One, two, three, Eagles win!"

Eleven guys ran onto the field. Keaton stayed on the sideline near the coach, hoping he would notice him and put him in the game. This was the first time Keaton could ever remember not being a starter. It was hard to just watch. He wanted to be out on the field, running around and making tackles.

Part of the problem was all his friends had grown a lot the last two years and Keaton had barely grown an inch.

"Don't sweat it," his dad said to him. "I had to wait for my growth spurt when I was your age too."

But those words weren't helping his discouragement now. It was hard to see guys pass him up for playing time. Keaton was working just as hard in practice as they were but wasn't doing quite as well.

At halftime, Keaton had only been in the game for a couple of plays. He was frustrated waiting for his name to be called. It helped that it was a very good game. The score was tied and both teams were playing very well. As the players ate oranges and drank water, the coach gave instructions for the second half. He then asked if anyone had something to say.

Before he could think, the words just blurted out of Keaton's mouth: "You're doing great, guys. You can definitely win this game."

The coach gave Keaton a nod and said to the rest of the team, "I think that's all we need to hear. Now let's go get them!"

Keaton was right. The guys were doing great and they did win the game. He got to play the last two series on offense with his team ahead by two touchdowns. He even got to run the ball twice.

After the game, the coach pulled Keaton aside and said: "Keaton, I want you to know how valuable you are to this team. I know you want to be on the field more. And I'll keep putting you in when I think the time is right. But even if you aren't on the first team this year, you are definitely first team with your attitude, and that is making this team better."

Did Keaton want to play more snaps? Definitely. But he knew he could help the team both on and off the field.

LIFE LESSON

Every great team has some very good players. But every great team also needs to have members with a great attitude, who lift the team up and encourage everyone in the heat of battle. Work as hard as you can to be a starter, but work just as hard at being an encourager!

VERSE TO REMEMBER

We should think about each other to see how we can encourage each other to show love and do good works. HEBREWS 10:24 ERV

TO TALK ABOUT

Who is the best encourager on your team? How does encouragement help make your team better? How can you be a better encourager?

SÍ, SEÑORITA!

DO YOU WELCOME NEW PEOPLE TO YOUR NEIGHBORHOOD, YOUR CHURCH, YOUR GROUP OF FRIENDS, YOUR TEAM?

Briana hopped out of the car and ran toward the soccer field. She was a few minutes late for practice. As she looked toward the field, she saw that the team was huddled around the coach and hadn't started practicing yet. When she arrived, the coach was saying, "I want everyone to welcome Claire. She just moved here with her family. Make sure you introduce yourself and make sure you help her feel welcome."

Claire turned a little red as the coach talked and didn't look up.

I wonder what it feels like to be the new kid, Briana wondered. She still lived with her family in the same house that they had been in since she was a baby.

"Okay, two quick laps around the field and then get back here for stretching," the coach yelled.

The girls started trotting around the field in a big clump. Briana looked back. Claire was hanging back a little. She looked a little bit uncertain about herself. Briana liked to be the first one back on the field but decided to slow down so she could run next to Claire.

"Where did you move from?" Briana asked.

"We've been living in California," Claire answered. "My dad is in the military so we've moved a lot."

"Where else did you live?" Briana asked.

"We were in Memphis for a couple years and then in Norfolk, Virginia. We lived in Spain for a couple years before Germany."

"Wow, did you learn to speak Spanish?" Briana asked.

"Sí, señorita!" Claire answered.

Both girls laughed at her answer.

The coach kept everyone busy for the next ninety minutes on drills and then a scrimmage. Briana couldn't help but notice that Claire was a really good player. She would be great to have on the team. Afterward, the coach blew the whistle and yelled to the girls, "That's all! Don't forget we have an early game on Saturday!"

Briana looked over at the parking lot. Her mom was just pulling in to pick her up. She grabbed her backpack and ball but stopped before running to the car. She saw Claire pulling her socks and shin guards off and stepping into a pair of flipflops.

"Hey Claire," Briana called. "I am really glad you are on the team. I hope you like it here."

"You don't know how good that is to hear," Claire said. "It's always so hard to move and make new friends. I'm glad I've already found one."

"You have for sure found a friend," Briana said. "I'll see you Saturday morning."

It made Briana feel good to know she had helped Claire find a friend and make her move easier.

LIFE LESSON

The best way to find a friend is to be a good friend. Don't wait for others to make the first move. Be the first one to introduce yourself and be friendly. It may make you a little nervous, but you will bless others and yourself when you do.

VERSE TO REMEMBER

Two people are better off than one, for they can help each other succeed. If one person falls, the other can reach out and help. But someone who falls alone is in real trouble.
ECCLESIASTES 4:9–10 NLT

TO TALK ABOUT

Have you ever moved and had to make friends? Do you know someone else who has? What is the hardest thing about making new friends? Are you willing to be the first one to be friendly?

SAYING "I'M SORRY" CAN BE HARD

ARE YOU WILLING TO MAKE THINGS RIGHT WHEN YOU HURT SOMEONE ELSE?

It was a total accident. No way did Keith mean to hurt Kevin, but he did.

The two were playing a one-on-one basketball game after team practice. Both Keith and Kevin were tired, but they loved to compete hard with each other to see who would win.

They were only playing a short game. The first one to get eleven points was the winner. The rule was "make it, take it," which meant if you made a basket, you got to keep the ball.

Keith started off hot. He hit his first five shots. But then he missed a short fall away jumper. He tried to use the backboard, but his angle was wrong, and the ball rolled around the rim before falling outside.

Kevin got even hotter than Keith. He hit his first six shots. When he finally missed, Keith grabbed the rebound, took the ball back behind the line, and put up a jumper that he was sure was going to go in the basket. It was close again but bounced out.

That meant Kevin had the ball again and he was still hot. First he drained a long range shot.

Nothing Keith could do about that. Next, Kevin faked a jump shot. When Keith went up in the air, he zipped past him for an easy layup. Now Kevin was ahead 8–5.

He decided to drive toward the basket for another layup. Keith was determined to block the shot. As the two boys went up in the air, their bodies slammed into each other. Keith landed on his feet. But Kevin fell in an awkward position. The snap of Kevin's ankle breaking was terrible to hear. Keith felt sick to his stomach. Kevin gave out a cry of pain as he clutched his injured foot.

Keith ran to the coach's office. He was a teacher at the school, so he was grading papers.

"Kevin's hurt!" Keith yelled.

The coach scrambled to his feet and ran out to the gym with Keith. After giving a quick examination, the coach reached into his pocket, pulled out his cell phone, and called Kevin's parents. He told them what had happened.

"I'm positive Kevin's ankle is broken. Do you want me to call an ambulance or do you want to take him to the emergency room yourselves?"

Kevin's family lived close to the school, so his parents picked him up and took to the hospital to get his bone set and put in a cast.

Keith felt terrible that he had caused his friend so much pain. He could barely eat dinner. He just looked down at his plate and moved the food around with his fork.

Keith's dad called Kevin's dad to see how Kevin was doing. Keith heard his dad say, "That's good news. And yes, we want to come over. We'll come by tomorrow."

All the next day at school, Keith walked around like he was in a daze. He wanted to go visit his friend to see how he was doing. But he was afraid, too. What if Kevin was mad at him? What if Kevin said that he hurt him on purpose? What if Kevin didn't want him to come visit?

When Keith and his dad stepped through the front door, Kevin was sitting in a big comfortable chair with his foot propped up on a footrest. He had a TV tray full of food on his lap and the TV remote control. There was a huge white cast on the bottom of his leg.

It was hard, but Keith stammered out, "I'm really sorry I hurt you, Kevin."

"No problem, man," Kevin answered with a smile. "I got to miss a day of school. I've been watching TV all day. And I bet I can get some girls to carry my books at school. The doc says I'll be fine in no time. I know you didn't hurt me on purpose."

Wow. That was a lot easier than Keith expected it to be. He knew he didn't purposely hurt Kevin, but he was glad he came over to say he was sorry.

LIFE LESSON

Don't wait! When you've hurt someone, on purpose or not, when you've done something wrong, get it taken care of immediately. Say you're sorry for a mistake. Ask for forgiveness for a sin. And move on with peace.

VERSE TO REMEMBER

Be kind to each other, tenderhearted, forgiving one another, just as God through Christ has forgiven you. EPHESIANS 4:32 NLT

TO TALK ABOUT

Is there someone you have hurt physically or with words? Are you ready to say you are sorry? Practice what you will say to that person.

PENALTY KICK

SOMETIMES ONE OF OUR TEAMMATES MAKES A BAD PLAY. IT'S EASY TO PLAY THE BLAME GAME. BUT IS THAT THE RIGHT ATTITUDE?

Lincoln was playing on a sports team for the very first time in his life. One of his good friends, Alan, kept telling him that he would really like playing soccer. Lincoln wasn't sure he wanted to play and missed the signup deadline. But since Alan's dad was coach of the Hornets, he was able to help Lincoln get on the team.

Since Lincoln had never played soccer before, he wasn't very good at dribbling the ball with his feet. A lot of things about playing soccer confused him. But he was tall and had quick reflexes. Alan's dad put Lincoln at goalie, and Lincoln was very good at it after just a few games.

The Hornets had a very good soccer season. They won eight games and only lost two. That meant they were one of the top four teams and got to play in the championship tournament.

In the first game, the Hornets played a team that had beat them the very first game of the regular season. This time the Hornets won. Lincoln stopped every shot from the other team. The coach, Alan's dad, said Lincoln was most valuable player!

In the finals, the game was tied when regulation

time was up. That meant both teams would get to shoot five penalty kicks. Alan scored the first goal for the Hornets. Two teammates missed and then two more scored for three points. Lincoln stopped the first penalty kick. The next three players scored. It was all tied up with one more kick. Lincoln knew he had to stop it. But even though he dove for the ball, it went into the back of the net for a goal. The Hornets had lost.

"I can't believe you missed that ball," one of Lincoln's teammates said to him. "You lost the game for us."

Lincoln felt terrible. He had let the team down. He wondered to himself why he agreed to play soccer on Alan's team.

Lincoln put his head down. Then he felt a hand on his shoulder. It was Coach.

"Lincoln, just so you know, I thought you played an incredible game. You are the most improved player I have ever coached. We could never have made it to the finals. I think you were the best goalie in the league."

Later, after the Hornets received their second-place medals, the kid who said "you lost the game for us" walked up to Lincoln and said, "I'm sorry for what I said earlier. You're an awesome goalie."

LIFE LESSON

Teams win together and lose together. It's never helpful to play the "blame game." Even if one of your teammates makes a mistake, be an encourager.

VERSE TO REMEMBER

So encourage each other and help each other grow stronger in faith, just as you are already doing.
I THESSALONIANS 5:11 ERV

TO TALK ABOUT

Who is someone who encouraged you when you didn't do as well as you wanted? How can you be an encourager?

TRIPPED!

HOW SHOULD YOU RESPOND WHEN OTHERS CHEAT AND DON'T PLAY BY THE RULES?

Megan was skating toward the goal. She kept her hockey stick low to the ice to control the slippery puck. As she pushed herself to go even faster, she looked ahead and saw the goalie crouched, ready to block her shot. One more skate forward and she raised her stick to slap a shot at the goal. Just as Megan was ready to unleash the shot, her right ankle was tugged backward. The next thing she knew, she was airborne. Megan landed on the ice with a thud. Her elbows and knees were on fire with pain.

A cry went up from the crowd of parents and friends. The referee blew his whistle and pointed at the girl who tripped Megan and then to the penalty box. He lifted two fingers and called out, "Two minutes."

Megan's coach motioned for her to skate to the bench.

"But it's not the end of my shift; I'm okay," Megan protested. "I'm not hurt that bad. I can keep playing."

"Take a breather and let's have someone look at your elbows," the coach said firmly. "Then we'll see if you can go back in and play some more."

Even though a trainer at the game checked on

Megan and said she could go back in with the next shift, the coach kept Megan out the rest of the game to be safe.

"You took a good fall and I want you to be completely healthy for next game," he said to her.

On the drive home with her mom, Megan didn't say anything. She stared straight ahead. She was furious. In her mind, she wanted to get revenge on the girl who tripped her. It wasn't an accident. She deliberately stuck her stick in front of Megan's ankle to trip her.

"What are you thinking, Megan?" her mom asked.

"I don't want to say," Megan answered.

"Can I guess what you don't want to say?" Mom asked her.

After a short pause, Megan finally admitted, "I just want to play against that girl again, so I can trip her back!"

"Do you think what that girl did to you was good?" Mom asked.

"No," Megan answered.

"Did you admire her?" Mom asked.

"No."

"So would it be good to do the same thing she did?"

"No," Megan said softly.

"So what can you do?" her mom asked.

"Nothing, I guess," Megan said.

"Are you sure?" Mom asked.

Megan thought for a moment. She wasn't nearly as angry as she was when she got in the car with her mom. She remembered a lesson her mom had told her many times: the best way to deal with a difficult person is to pray for them.

"I can pray for her," Megan said. "But I'm still mad at her."

Megan's mom laughed and said, "Once you start praying for her, you won't be mad much longer."

LIFE LESSON

We show others that we have Jesus in our heart when we forgive and love—even those that hurt us.

VERSE TO REMEMBER

But I tell you, love your enemies. Pray for those who treat you badly. MATTHEW 5:44 ERV

TO TALK ABOUT

Have you ever been really mad at someone who hurt you? Did you want to get back at them? Have you prayed for that person?

THE MUD BOWL

SOME DIRT AND MUD WON'T EVER COME OUT OF A UNIFORM. BUT WHAT ABOUT OUR HEARTS?

Jeremy could hardly fall asleep thinking about what was coming up the next day. It was the last game of the season. Bruins versus Cowboys. The winner would have the best record in the city youth league. Every time the Bruins and Cowboys played, a big crowd showed up, because everyone knew it would be a great game.

Jeremy was out of bed early. His dad didn't have to wake him up like most Saturday mornings. He jumped out of bed and bounded down the stairs to get a bowl of cereal. He was thinking he might have two bowls since he would need his energy for the game.

As he got to the bottom of the stairs and turned into the kitchen, his eyes got wide and his jaw dropped open. He looked out the window and saw nothing but rain. His dad looked up from his newspaper, took a sip of coffee, and smiled.

"Dad! It's game day. They aren't going to cancel the game because of a little rain, are they?"

"So far, the game is on," his dad answered. "No lightning has been spotted. The city has already scheduled to put down new seed on the fields next week. So it doesn't matter how muddy the field gets. I think we're on, Jeremy. Now your mom has already told me that there's no way she is going to sit in that pouring rain all morning. Are you sure you want to play in a flood?"

He was. But by halfway through the game he wasn't so sure about his answer. Jeremy was running back for the Bruins. But with all the rain, he had fumbled the wet, slimy football four times. That was more than all his other games combined. The bad news was the Cowboys recovered three of those fumbles. But Jeremy wasn't the only one having troubles. The Cowboys' running back had fumbled five times. Both teams dropped a bunch of passes.

Jeremy looked at his uniform. It was soaked all the way through. You couldn't even tell that his pants were white anymore, they were so covered with mud. Every time he took a step, it was like the mud was trying to pull one of his shoes off. Every time he was off the field, he would get a rag and try to clean the mud from his facemask.

The two teams fought back and forth but no one could score in the mud. When the horn sounded to end the game, Jeremy was hoping the referees would let them play overtime. No such luck. The rain was coming down even harder, so the game ended in a 0–0 tie.

"Did you have fun, Jeremy?" his dad asked as they walked toward the car.

"It was a blast," Jeremy said. "But I don't think it was a very good football game."

"It was a great game," his dad said with a smile. "You just played in the muddiest game I have ever seen. But you're not getting in the car until I put towels down on the seats. You need to get those muddy cleats off and I'll put them in the trunk."

"Do you think my uniform will ever get clean again?" Jeremy asked.

His dad looked him up and down, shook his head, and said with a frown, "Son, those mud stains are never coming out. Nothing is going to get your uniform clean again."

Jeremy and his dad talked on the way home. As they pulled into their neighborhood, Jeremy's dad said, "Even if your uniform won't ever look clean again, you need to know that if you do the wrong thing and sin, God's love and forgiveness can make even the muddiest heart clean again. All you have to do is ask for forgiveness and really mean it."

Jeremy thought about that for a minute and then asked, "Is that why God sent Jesus?"

His dad nodded and said, "You are exactly right, son. There's something a lot more important than a uniform that needs to be made new and clean again."

LIFE LESSON

All of us have fallen short of God's perfect plan for our life. All of us have gotten our heart and soul dirty through disobedience and sin. The wonderful news is that God offers us forgiveness. We must be sorry for our sins. We must ask Him to forgive us of our sins. We must trust that He will cleanse us and help us to do the right thing next time.

VERSE TO REMEMBER

Remove my sin and make me pure. Wash me until I am whiter than snow! PSALM 51:7 ERV

TO TALK ABOUT

Are you sorry for the times you have sinned? Have you told God you are sorry? Have you asked Him to forgive you? Are you ready to pray today?

BLOCKED SHOT

**NOT EVERYTHING GOES OUR WAY.
SOMETIMES WE FACE
DISAPPOINTMENTS IN LIFE.
THE IMPORTANT THING IS
TO STAY POSITIVE AND
KEEP MOVING FORWARD.**

Breanna's face was bright red. She was so embarrassed. How could a game go so badly?

She was the tallest girl on her basketball team. She played center. She was the leading scorer and rebounder for her team. And her team was quite good.

But now the Cougars were getting beaten badly and Breanna couldn't seem to do anything right. The problem was that the other team's center was even taller than Breanna. Every time a teammate passed the ball to Breanna, she would turn to score, just like she always did. But the other girl kept blocking her shot.

With only three minutes to go, Breanna finally scored her first points. Jenn lobbed the pass in to her. She turned quickly, dribbled the ball twice, and made an easy layup. She took a deep breath and sighed. Breanna was relieved she had made at least one basket.

The problem was the other team was winning

by so many points that the other center was sitting on the bench.

The other coach probably feels sorry for me, Breanna thought to herself.

After the game, Breanna got in line and high fived the other team. The last girl she came to was the other center.

"Good game," the girl said to Breanna.

"You had a great game," Breanna responded. "You are way too good for me."

"I've been playing since I was barely able to walk," the girl said nicely. "My dad played basketball a long time, so he always wanted his kids to play too. How long have you been playing?"

"This is my second year," Breanna answered.

"Well, by the time we get to school ball, you'll probably catch up to me. You're really doing great. Maybe we'll be on the same team one day."

"I hope so," Breanna exclaimed with a laugh. "It's too hard playing against you!"

Breanna felt good that the other girl had taken time to talk with her and say some nice things. She was still very disappointed in how badly her team got beat. She was also still very embarrassed at how many times her shot got blocked.

Later, at home, she realized wasn't disappointed anymore. That surprised her. She usually felt lousy until the next day if she had a bad game.

What was different? Breanna realized that

instead of being discouraged and disappointed, she felt determined to practice harder and get better. She hopped off the couch to head outside and shoot some hoops on the driveway. With no one else around, at least she wouldn't get any more shots blocked, she thought with a smile.

LIFE LESSON

Every single one of us will face disappointments, not just in sports but in other areas of life. When life doesn't go our way, that doesn't mean we are defeated. It means we need to turn to God in prayer. He will give us joy and strength to keep trying.

VERSE TO REMEMBER

Always be filled with joy in the Lord. I will say it again. Be filled with joy. Let everyone see that you are gentle and kind. The Lord is coming soon. Don't worry about anything, but pray and ask God for everything you need, always giving thanks for what you have. PHILIPPIANS 4:4–6 ERV

TO TALK ABOUT

How do you respond when you face a disappointment? Do you get angry? Do you get sad? What can you do next time something doesn't go right to honor God and grow stronger?

GOTTA WORK TOGETHER!

IN SPORTS, WE PUT IN A LOT OF INDIVIDUAL EFFORT. BUT TO BE SUCCESSFUL, WE MUST ALSO WORK WELL WITH OTHERS.

Eli was nervous. His team had loaded up in a couple of vans this morning to drive to a big regional track meet. Track was a lot of fun for Eli. He didn't always like the running workouts, but he was fast and did well. His coach was very funny, and he liked him a lot. His coach had been a track star in college so he knew a lot of tips to help the team run faster, jump higher, and throw farther.

Eli knew only a couple of the other kids before he joined the team, but now it seemed like everyone on the team was a best friend. When his mom asked what his favorite part of being on the track team was, Eli's answer was easy: "My friends."

Eli was a sprinter. He and one other guy on the team, Garon, were almost the exact same speed. Sometimes Garon would get the gold medal and Eli would get the silver medal. Sometimes Eli would get the gold. The two boys were part of the 4x1 sprint team that had a chance to take first place in this track meet.

Eli knew his team was fast enough to win.

117

What made him nervous was handing off the baton. If they dropped the baton even one time, there was no way they could take first. Eli was the fourth runner this meet. Garon would be handing the baton to him. But a couple times in practice the past week he had dropped the baton. Was it because Garon wasn't putting it in his hand right? Or was it because he wasn't holding his hand back right? Or was he thinking about running as fast as he could and not concentrating?

Now Eli's heart was pounding. He and Garon had to get this right. The gun had sounded. The first runner on his team started off fast. He was the second runner to hand off the baton. The exchange went perfectly. The second runner was in the lead when he handed it to Garon. Eli watched as Garon blazed toward him. They could definitely win. All he needed to do was take the baton from Garon cleanly.

Eli started moving forward as Garon drove his legs forward. Garon raised the baton. Eli reached back. He almost yelled with joy as he raced toward the finish line with the baton securely in his hand.

Eli crossed the line three steps ahead of the second place team. They had won! His coach was beaming. Eli looked up in the stands. His mom was yelling louder than anyone. He smiled.

His first thought was, *I did it!* But as Garon walked up to him, breathing hard and smiling, Eli realized he hadn't done it by himself. The whole team had done it.

"We did it!" Eli yelled.

LIFE LESSON

Think about how to be your very best in sports, in school, at home, and with friends. But never forget that we need the help and encouragement of others to be at our best.

VERSE TO REMEMBER

We should think about each other to see how we can encourage each other to show love and do good works. We must not quit meeting together, as some are doing. No, we need to keep on encouraging each other. This becomes more and more important as you see the Day getting closer.
HEBREWS 10:24–25 ERV

TO TALK ABOUT

Who is the biggest encourager in your life? What do they say or do to help you do better? Who can you encourage? How can you be a better teammate?

MY LEFT FOOT

**ALL OF US HAVE THINGS
WE ARE GOOD AT AND THINGS WE ARE
NOT VERY GOOD AT. WHAT SHOULD
YOU DO WITH YOUR WEAKNESSES?**

My name is Beverly and I play soccer. I'm a forward. I'm quite fast. I can kick the ball as hard as anyone in my age group. My problem is I can only kick hard and dribble good with my right foot. For some reason, my left foot won't cooperate. I practice with it. I shoot at the goal with only my left foot at least twenty-five times before practice starts. I make myself dribble around the field with only my left foot after practice—at least until my dad honks the horn to let me know it is time to go. But it still isn't very strong.

My mom told me not to worry about it. She said that none of us are good at everything. When I told that to my coach, she smiled, and wrote down some extra practice drills I can do at home.

I do them every day but it's just not working.

I told my teacher at school about my left foot. She laughed and then got serious. She said, "Beverly, I think you are worrying about your left foot too much. Stop thinking about your left foot all the time and I bet it will start doing better."

I tried not to think about my left foot. But every time I tried not to think about it, I ended up thinking about it. That strategy didn't work very well for me.

One of my friends at church said she would pray for my left foot. I know we should pray about everything and I know God answers our prayers. But so far, His answer has been, "No." My left foot still isn't doing very good in games.

I have to admit, my left foot is making me mad. I look at both of my feet very closely. They are both the same size. My legs are the same length. So why can my right foot kick the ball so hard and my left can barely get the soccer ball off the ground? I can pass the ball right to my teammates with my right foot. With my left foot, my passes are never very accurate. I finally got so mad that I yelled at my left foot. My dad walked in right when I was yelling. He started laughing at me and told me I was acting strange. I think he was right.

I talked to my mom last night at bedtime. She told me to be patient. She said that in some areas of life, it just takes time to grow. She told me that when she was growing up, her family always went to restaurants for meals, so it took her a long time to get good at cooking when she married dad.

That finally made me smile. She asked what I thought was so funny.

I finally had to admit that she still isn't very good at cooking. We both laughed when I said that.

So maybe some day my left foot will wake up and do what I want it to do. Until then, I guess I'll have to be patient.

LIFE LESSON

We can't be good at everything we do. God doesn't want us to get mad at ourselves. He wants us to be patient and keep growing. Most of all, God wants us to know that He loves us just the way we are.

VERSE TO REMEMBER

I praise you because you made me in such a wonderful way. I know how amazing that was! PSALM 139:14 ERV

TO TALK ABOUT

What are some things you are good at doing? What are some things that you wish you did better? Have you thanked God for making you the way you are?

A HELPING HAND

WHICH IS MORE IMPORTANT: GOOD SPORTSMANSHIP OR WINNING?

Monica hit a hard line drive down the third base line. No way could the left fielder get to the ball before it went to the wall. The left fielder ran as fast as she could to reach the ball while Monica ran as hard as she could to turn her hit into a triple or maybe even a home run.

The ball hit the outfield fence at an angle and bounced in a different direction than the outfielder was running. She had to change directions. Monica saw this happening as she rounded second base. Her heart soared. Maybe she would get her first ever home run.

Monica ran as hard as she could and kept her eyes forward. Her third base coach was waving his arm in circles and yelling, "Keep running! Keep running! Keep running!"

Sure enough, Monica was going to try and beat the throw and get a home run.

As she rounded third, Monica could see her friends jumping up and down in the dugout. They were excited and cheering her on.

Then it happened.

As Monica planted her left foot to make her final charge for home plate, her ankle turned outward. Pain shot up and down her left foot and leg as she fell to the ground. Tears immediately popped from her eyes. Even as she let out a sob, she heard the crowd at the game groan and then go very quiet.

Her coach ran over to her and put a hand on her shoulder.

"Don't move, Monica. Just take it easy. Let's take a look at that ankle."

Even as she sobbed, Monica wanted to crawl down the base path and finish her hit. She didn't want to be out. She wanted that home run. She wanted to help her team win. But her ankle hurt so bad, all she could do was cry.

A small group of adults huddled around her, including a doctor who came down from the stands. Keeping her foot very still, he had Monica turn over and sit up so she could look at her injured ankle.

"I'm pretty sure it's not broken," the doctor said, "but she needs to keep weight of it and go get an x-ray."

Monica's coach bent down to pick her up. But then something incredible happened. Two of the girls on the other team bent down. They each put one of Monica's arms over their shoulder. They then walked her to home plate, being careful not to let her injured ankle touch the ground. Once there, Monica stepped on home plate. The other team had held the ball so she was safe. She had hit her first home run.

Monica looked at one of the girls and asked, "Why did you do that for me?"

"Helping a friend who is hurt is more important than winning."

Even with the pain, Monica felt a strong surge of gratitude.

LIFE LESSON

It's great to compete hard. It's great to win. But sometimes we have to forget about winning and help someone who is hurt.

VERSE TO REMEMBER

Feel sorry for hungry people and give them food. Help those who are troubled and satisfy their needs. Then your light will shine in the darkness. You will be like the bright sunshine at noon. The Lord will always lead you and satisfy your needs in dry lands. He will give strength to your bones. You will be like a garden that has plenty of water, like a spring that never goes dry.
ISAIAH 58:10–11 ERV

TO TALK ABOUT

What should you do when a friend gets hurt? What are ways you can help others who have special needs?

HAPPY, HAPPY, HAPPY

IS IT POSSIBLE TO BE HAPPY BOTH WHEN WE WIN AND WHEN WE LOSE?

Noah didn't really like baseball or basketball. He especially didn't like football.

His best friend, Liam, would give him a hard time and ask, "What in the world is the matter with you, Noah? How can you not love football?"

Noah tried swimming and diving. He loved being in the water but just wasn't very good at either. He played a couple of seasons of soccer, but he wasn't crazy about that either. Noah liked physical exercise. He was plenty strong and fast. Since most of his friends played at least one sport, he wondered if something was wrong with him.

Then he got a lacrosse set from one of his uncles for his birthday. He opened the package and pulled out the helmet, the shoulder pads, the arm pads, the gloves, the ball, and two sticks. He gave his uncle a big hug and immediately called Liam.

"Come over to my backyard right away," Noah said. "You won't believe what I just got from my uncle."

Liam came over and the two boys passed the ball back and forth, while running all over the yard. Noah's dog, Bobby, had almost as much fun as Noah and Liam. He chased them the whole time and tried to run off with the ball whenever one of the boys would drop it.

Two months later, a new lacrosse season started up at the YMCA. Noah reminded his parents a hundred times to make sure they signed him up.

After a couple weeks of practice, Noah played his first game. It was the most fun he had ever had playing sports. Most of the guys on his team were as new to lacrosse as Noah was. The other team had a number of players that had been in lacrosse for two or even three years. Noah's team got beaten very badly.

On the drive home, Noah's mom said to him, "You sure don't seem very upset that your team lost. Do you feel a little bad?"

"No way!" Noah said. "I finally found a sport I love. I know we're not very good yet, but my team will get better and better. I will too."

"Well, that's a wonderful way to think about it, Noah," his mom said. "It sure gave you a lot of energy out on the field. I've never seen you run so fast."

"I'm not happy because of what I'm thinking, I'm happy because of what I'm feeling," Noah responded. "My heart is happy, happy, happy."

"Well, you keep smiling, Noah," Mom said. "It's contagious. I'm getting the very same feeling of happiness."

LIFE LESSON

Whether we win or lose, with God inside of us and beside us, we can always choose to be joyful. Joy comes from inside us, no matter what is happening around us.

VERSE TO REMEMBER

You will teach me the right way to live. Just being with you will bring complete happiness. Being at your right side will make me happy forever. PSALM 16:11 ERV

TO TALK ABOUT

What things have made you sad and unhappy? Do you know that God is with you even when things don't turn out right? Have you ever asked God to give you joy?

THE JUMP

HOW DO WE RESPOND WHEN SOMEONE DOES BETTER THAN US?

I took my tape measure and made a chalk mark twelve feet from the center and twenty feet back from the high jump bar.

During warm-ups, I made sure to push off hard with my first step. I kept my back straight. I stayed as tall as I could as I ran. I made my turn at the same spot every time and planted hard with my left foot.

My goal was to hit 5'10", which would be a record for fifth graders at my school. My friend Eddie was doing the same warm-up as me. He didn't usually do real well, but I was hoping he had a good day. Maybe he could get up to 5'4" or something good.

My coach told me not to jump at the first two heights. He didn't want me to get worn out jumping at easy heights for me. I looked over at Eddie. He made the first two heights on his first attempts.

"Great job, Eddie!" I yelled.

"Thanks, Sammy!" he yelled back.

I took my first jump at 5'2" and made it easy. So did Eddie.

At 5'4" there were only four of us left. Me, Eddie, and two guys from other teams, Derek and Levi. On the first round of jumps, all of us missed.

On the second round, only I made the jump. On the third round, Derek and Levi missed, but Eddie made it. That was his best jump ever. That left only two of us, both from the same team, in the high jump competition. I was really happy Eddie was doing so good.

At 5'6", Eddie and I both missed our first two jumps. That meant we only had one more chance. As I lined up, Eddie yelled encouragement: "You can do it, Sammy. You got this."

I pushed off hard and approached the bar. I lifted off hard with my left foot. It felt great. As I landed on the foam mat, the bar followed me, bonking me on the head. I couldn't believe it. I had barely touched the bar with my ankle and it fell.

As disappointed as I was, I knew I would still be the winner because Eddie had more jumps than me. That was the tiebreaker when jumpers finished at the same height. I gave Eddie a smile and thumbs-up as he lined up for his final jump.

He started his approach. He made his turn. He went up off his left foot. And to my amazement, he cleared the bar. He had just won the meet.

I felt a surge of sudden anger. This wasn't fair. No way was Eddie as good a jumper as me. I got unlucky with my ankle barely touching the bar. He got lucky with his best jump ever. I should be the champion!

As he popped off the foam mat, Eddie ran over with a huge smile on his face. He was high fiving everyone as he ran. But he gave me a huge bear hug and lifted me off the ground.

"I couldn't have done it without you, Sammy. You're almost as good of a coach as Coach! You're still the best, but I won one!"

How could I stay mad? He won fair and square. He had a great day and I had just an okay day, but I would have more chances. I still felt mad that I didn't do better but I worked hard to feel happy for Eddie.

LIFE LESSON

Sometimes it's easier to feel bad when others feel bad than it is to feel happy when others feel happy. It might be because of jealousy. Or maybe because of resentment. You show God's love when you celebrate with others' successes.

VERSE TO REMEMBER

When others are happy, you should be happy with them. And when others are sad, you should be sad too. ROMANS 12:15 ERV

TO TALK ABOUT

Have you ever felt a little mad at someone because of something good that happened to them? Have you ever been jealous and not felt happy when good things happen to others? What can you do the next time you feel this way?

OVERTIME

HOW DO YOU KEEP PUSHING WHEN YOU FEEL TOO TIRED TO MOVE?

At the end of the first quarter the game was tied 6–6. I had missed two shots but made two free throw shots to help the team.

We were playing against another team that was our archrival. The stands were full. My dad even took off work early to come see our last game of the season.

At the end of the second quarter, the game was tied 13–13. One of my teammates missed a shot but I got the rebound and scored an easy layup. So I was still helping the team.

The game was tough. There was a bunch of bumping. The referees were keeping a close eye on fouls, so their whistles kept blowing as they called fouls. I scored two more free throws in the third quarter. I did a head fake and a girl jumped on me. The problem was we were getting called for a lot of fouls too.

We started the fourth quarter tied 18–18. Just a minute in, my best friend, Sarah, tried to steal a ball and was whistled for her fifth foul. She was out of the game. A couple minutes later, Darlene tried to block a shot and fouled the girl. It was her fifth. She was out of the game too. I hadn't come out for even a minute of the game and was getting tired. But with two starters out, I might have to play to the very end.

The other team had two girls foul out, but with one minute left, it got even worse for us. A third starter, Pearl, got her fifth foul. She was out. This really was a rough game. The girl on the other team made both free throws and they took a two-point lead with thirty seconds to go.

The ball came to me and I dribbled down the floor. I looked left and right. Then I saw Teresa break for the basket. I threw a bounce pass that got there at just the right time. She scored to tie the game. The other team rushed the ball down the floor but missed a shot at the buzzer. We were going into overtime. I looked over at Coach to let her know I needed a rest. That was when I saw Teresa was hurt. The trainer took off her shoe. She wasn't going to be playing anymore. I was the last starter eligible to play.

I looked up at the stands. My parents were clapping for me. Dad yelled, "You can do it, Ava! You can do it!"

I didn't think I could. But I did. I scored two baskets in overtime. I made a steal. I got two rebounds. We still lost but I had gone a lot harder and longer than I thought I could. I was too tired to feel upset. I just shook hands, grabbed my bags, and headed for the car with my parents.

"You gotta be wiped out," Dad said.

"I can barely move," I answered.

"How did you do it, Ava?" Mom asked.

"Knowing the team needed me so bad helped me keep pushing," I said. "The crowd gave me some energy. Thanks for coming, Dad."

"I wouldn't have missed it for the world," he said.

"But most of all, I said a prayer. I think God gave me some extra energy, even if we didn't win."

"It sounds like you won to me," Mom said as she turned to smile at me.

LIFE LESSON

It can be very hard to keep working and pushing sometimes. We get tired. Our brains don't want to think about homework. Our bodies don't want to keep running. But we usually have more energy in the tank than we think to do. And most importantly, in our spiritual life, God gives us all the power and energy we need to keep going.

VERSE TO REMEMBER

But those who trust in the Lord will become strong again. They will be like eagles that grow new feathers. They will run and not get weak. They will walk and not get tired. ISAIAH 40:31 ERV

TO TALK ABOUT

When was a time you were in a game that you got so tired you wanted to stop? When was a time at school when you didn't want to do your work? Do you believe God can help you be stronger with your determination?

FRIENDS FOREVER

WHAT DO YOU DO WHEN YOUR BEST FRIEND IS ON THE OTHER TEAM?

Margie and Megan were best friends. They lived in the same neighborhood and could be found together at each other's houses quite often. Their parents were good friends. They went to the same school and had the same teacher. They went to the same church.

But they had one big difference. Margie played for the Rangers and Megan played for the Thunder. Somehow, they had not ended up on the same softball team. But both pitched and played first base. Both were good fielders and good hitters. Both were the best player on their team. But Margie wore a maroon and yellow uniform, and Megan wore a red and black uniform.

How would they respond when they played against each other? They would soon find out as the Rangers and Thunder were playing the third game of the season. Margie would be pitching. Megan had pitched the previous game, so she would be playing first base.

The game was tied 2–2 going into the last inning. Margie was still pitching. She had struck Megan out two times and walked her once. Now with two outs, and the game about to go into extra innings, Megan was back up at the plate. Her Thunder team had one girl on third base.

Margie's first pitch was high. Ball one. Her second pitch was outside the plate. Ball two. Her third pitch was a fast ball down the middle. Megan swung hard and fouled it back into the stands. Strike one. Margie's third pitch was close and the umpire called it a strike. Megan looked back at the ump with a scowl, but didn't complain. Her coach had a strict rule that players couldn't complain about calls.

With two outs and a two-two pitch count, Margie wound up. Her arm reached back and high. It moved lightning fast downward and forward as she threw a screaming fast ball.

Megan's eyes narrowed. Her weight shifted to her back foot. She drew the bat back. As the ball left Margie's hand, Megan was already starting her swing. The ping of aluminum bat hitting the softball was loud as she slammed the ball into the gap between left field and center field. The girl on third ran home easily. The Thunder won. Margie had given up the winning run to her best friend, Megan.

Both Margie and Megan's parents watched to see how the girls would handle facing each other in the game. The girls gave each other a hug and then trotted over to where their parents were talking.

"Can Margie spend the night?" Megan asked her mom.

"Sure," she answered. "But only after you two get all that dirt and dust cleaned off."

The girls laughed and ran off to talk to some of their other friends.

"I guess you can try your very best to beat each other on the field and still be great friends," Margie's dad said with a laugh.

LIFE LESSON

When we play sports, it feels like war sometimes. We want to win so bad, it's easy to look at the other team as the enemy. It's great to do our best to win, but we definitely shouldn't hate or dislike others just because they have a different colored uniform than we wear.

VERSE TO REMEMBER

And if you are nice only to your friends, you are no better than anyone else. Even the people who don't know God are nice to their friends. MATTHEW 5:47 ERV

TO TALK ABOUT

Have you ever wanted to hate someone because they played for another team? How hard is it to compete against a good friend?

KEEP YOUR HEAD UP

SPORTS TEACH US THE IMPORTANCE OF PAYING ATTENTION AND KEEPING OUR EYES OPEN AND ALERT.

My dad played football all the way from grade school to middle school to high school to college to the pros. He only played professional football for two years, but he was good enough to make it. In our upstairs bonus room, there is a trophy case filled with silver awards he has won.

I'm very proud of my dad. He is a good dad in all ways. He makes sure I do my homework. He takes us to church every week. He says a prayer with me almost every night. He is also a great coach who helps me do very good in football. That is my favorite sport by far. I would love to go to the same college as him as a football player when I get older.

One of the things my dad always tells me is to keep my eyes and head up:

"You gotta keep your eyes and head up. Doesn't matter how fast you are. Doesn't matter how hard you tackle. Doesn't matter how good you run the ball or catch the ball or pass the ball. You gotta keep your eyes and head up. That's how you make the right play. That's how you keep from making mistakes. That's how you keep from getting yourself hurt."

I knew my dad was right. Most of the times I listened to him. But one game, my team was getting beat. Nothing was going right for us. I was playing on the left side, so the other team kept running to the right side. They kept gaining big chunks of yardage on long runs. I was getting mad because I wasn't making any tackles. No one was running in my direction. We were losing by two touchdowns at the end of the third quarter. We still had time to win the game, but it was getting desperate. The other team had the ball and was driving again. I knew they would run to the right. As soon as the ball was snapped, the quarterback handed the ball off, and sure enough, the running back took off to the right.

We had to get a stop so I took off running to that side of the field as hard as I could. I was going to make the tackle so we could get the ball back. But the running back flipped the ball to the wide receiver. He was running the other way. He was running to the left side of the field. And because I had taken off across the field, without keeping my eye on where the ball was, there was no one left to tackle him. The wide receiver ran for an easy touchdown.

I looked up in the stands at my dad. He was pointing two fingers at his eyes. I knew exactly what he was thinking: "You gotta keep your head up and your eyes open."

I wanted to make a good play so bad. I gave it

my best effort. But I made a huge mistake by not knowing where the ball was.

That was the game I learned my lesson. To be a great player, you have to know what is going on around you. You have to keep your head up and your eyes open.

LIFE LESSON

In sports we learn to play "smart." We learn that we can't just use our bodies, we have to use our head to play good. In our spiritual life, we learn that we need to keep our mind and eyes on what is most important. Nothing is more important than keeping our eyes and mind on Jesus. He shows us the best way we can live.

VERSE TO REMEMBER

We must never stop looking to Jesus. He is the leader of our faith, and he is the one who makes our faith complete. He suffered death on a cross. But he accepted the shame of the cross as if it were nothing because of the joy he could see waiting for him. And now he is sitting at the right side of God's throne. HEBREWS 12:2 ERV

TO TALK ABOUT

How do we keep our mind and eyes on Jesus? What can you do to stay focused on Him?

THE RACE

TO WIN A RACE, WE CAN'T JUST START FAST, WE HAVE TO FINISH FAST. WHAT DOES IT TAKE TO RUN FAST ALL THE WAY TO THE END?

Every year my school hosts a big outdoor game meet for elementary schools in our town. It is called the Highland Games. Highland is the name of our city.

There are a lot of track events but also some events that our PE teacher added. We have a softball throw to see who can throw the farthest. We have sack races and wheelbarrow races. We even have an egg toss, to see what two people can throw back and forth to each other without breaking the egg.

My favorite event every year is the mile run. Most kids my age think running a mile is awful. It seems like a punishment to them, not something that is a lot of fun. For me, it is great. I run to and from school every day. It is almost a mile each way. So I get lots of practices. Other kids take the bus or have a parent drive them to school. I like to run.

One of my good friends, Benjamin, says he is going to beat me in the mile this year.

"No way," I said to Benjamin.

"Keaton, this is the year I am going to beat you," he said.

I don't know how he can think he has a chance against me. I'm not bragging. But I run every day. Benjamin never runs. He takes the bus to school every day. When he gets home, he likes to play video games instead of come outside and play ball.

On the day of the Highland Games, Benjamin had a big smile.

"I'm going to beat you this year, Keaton!"

I just smiled back.

"We'll see," was all I said.

We had a fun day. My school was getting the most points. The last event was the mile run. Benjamin and I lined up next to each other. When the gun sounded, we took off side by side.

For the first half mile, Benjamin kept up with me. I was really impressed. But the second half of the race, he couldn't keep up. I finished in third place. As I walked around with my hands on my head, trying to get more air into my lungs, Benjamin finally crossed the finish line. He looked like he was ready to throw up and faint.

I walked over and said, "Good job, Benjamin. You really ran great."

"But I didn't beat you this year," he groaned. "How do you keep running so fast for a whole mile?"

"Easy," I said with a laugh. "I practice and train. You could do the same thing, but you have to get out and run every day."

LIFE LESSON

Many people want to have success without working hard to earn it. Whatever sport you play requires practice and training. In the same way, your spiritual life requires training. We need to read God's Word, pray, serve others, and spend time with other Christians.

VERSE TO REMEMBER

Training your body helps you in some ways. But devotion to God helps you in every way. It brings you blessings in this life and in the future life too. I TIMOTHY 4:8 ERV

TO TALK ABOUT

Are you training yourself to be strong spiritually? What are some ways you can grow spiritually stronger?

RED CARD!

RULES ARE MADE TO KEEP GAMES FAIR AND SAFE.

Beau was a very good soccer player. The problem was the number of penalties he got. He never tried to cheat or hurt someone, he just had a habit of running into other players when he ran for the ball.

"Beau, I like the way you play so hard," his coach said to him, "but you got to play smarter. You know the rules. It is okay to 'shoulder in' on another player. But you can't just run into people, especially if you are behind them. It hurts the team when you get so many penalties."

On his team's first travel tournament, Beau's coach went over the tournament rules with them. He looked right at Beau when he said, "If a player gets a second yellow card during the tournament, that means the player automatically gets a red card. The team will play with one less player the rest of the game. And not only will you be out for the rest of the game, but you'll have to sit out the next game too."

In the first game of the tournament, Beau played fast and smart. He had a couple of bumps with other players, but everything was fair and by the rules. No one received a yellow card. No one got hurt.

In the second game, Beau and a player from another team raced for the ball. Beau thought he got to the ball a half-step ahead of the other player. When they bumped into each other, the other player took a tumble and did a somersault after falling. Beau was positive he got there first, but the referee pulled out a yellow card and pointed to him.

Uh-oh. What if he got another yellow card? The coach had read the tournament rules. That would mean an automatic red card. That would mean his team would play with one less player and he would have to sit on the bench the next game too.

In the third round, Beau's team was tied. If they won the game, they would advance to the championship round. If they lost, they would be done with the tournament. Beau was playing midfield. The goalie on the other team cleared the ball wide. Beau saw his chance. If he got to the ball first, he would be in an excellent scoring position. It was a race between him and a defender from the other team. As he closed in on the ball, Beau realized the other player was going to get to it first. He wanted so badly to push harder and see if he could win the race. But at the last second, Beau slowed down, took a step back, and went on defense as the other player controlled the ball.

Later in the game, Beau's team scored a goal to win the game and advance to the championship round. When the team huddled up afterward, Beau's coach looked at him and said:

"I'm proud of you, Beau. You played hard and smart. If you had gone after that one ball and knocked the other kid down, you would have got a red card. No way could we have won. I'm glad you played smart."

LIFE LESSON

Go hard as you can on the sports field and every other area of your life. Try hard. Compete hard. Play to win. But don't forget the rules. Rules keep the game fair and the players safe!

VERSE TO REMEMBER

If you fail to do what you know is right, you are sinning. JAMES 4:17 ERV

TO TALK ABOUT

What are some important rules in your family? At your school? On your sports team? What rules are hardest to follow? Why does God want us to follow rules in life?

DIVE FOR IT!

THE MOST IMPORTANT THING IN SPORTS IS FOR YOU TO GIVE YOUR BEST.

Ginger played middle row as setter for her volleyball team. She knew other girls were bigger, stronger, and quicker, but her goal was to be the number-one hustler. Every player wore knee and elbow pads, but no other player needed them more than Ginger.

She would dive to try and pop up a hard spike from the other team. If a ball bounced high in the air off the court, Ginger would still rush over to try and save it. One time she even dove into the stands to try and get a ball. She landed on the lap of someone's grandpa. He had a long white beard and was very round. Everyone teased her that she was sitting on Santa's lap.

Ginger just laughed. She didn't mind getting teased. She knew that the best way she could help her team was by being the world's greatest hustler.

"You're going to get hurt diving for the ball all the time," her teammate Sandra said to her. "Plus the other team usually gets the point anyway."

Ginger thought about that. Was Sandra right? Was she just being crazy by diving for every ball?

But the next match, in the final game, Ginger did what she always did. A girl from the other team hit a hard spike. It bounced off the arm of one of her teammates and headed toward the back wall. Sandra sprinted hard. She dove for the ball and got her arms under it. The ball went flying high back toward the court. Sandra got to it first. She sent the ball over to the other side of the net. The same girl tried another spike, but this time the ball went outside the court. Ginger had saved the day with her hustle. Her team had won.

As the girls jumped around and celebrated, Sandra came over to Ginger and gave her a big hug.

"You may be a little crazy, Ginger, but keep being crazy. You just won the game for us!"

LIFE LESSON

Just because we try hard doesn't mean we will automatically win the game or get an A on a test or make the best project for science fair. But trying hard and giving our best sets up us for success in all areas of life. It is showing faithfulness to God's gifts to us.

VERSES TO REMEMBER

In all the work you are given, do the best you can. Work as though you are working for the Lord, not any earthly master. Remember that you will receive your reward from the Lord, who will give you what he promised his people. Yes, you are serving Christ. He is your real Master.
COLOSSIANS 3:23–24 ERV

TO TALK ABOUT

Has there been a time when you didn't try hard? How did that make you feel? When you try hard, how does that make you feel? Why is it so important to give our best effort?

FIRST THINGS FIRST

WHAT IS MOST IMPORTANT TO YOU?
IS GOD FIRST IN YOUR LIFE?

Sports are great. But the most important thing in your life is not how good you are at...

Volleyball
Baseball
Football
Basketball
Gymnastics
Skateboarding
Tennis
Lacrosse
Cheerleading
Wrestling

...Or any other sport you play!

School is important. Getting good grades is important. But that's not what is most important in your life.

Friendship is also very important. But being popular and getting along with others is not what is most important for you.

156

What matters most? Knowing how much God loves you and loving Him with all your heart, mind, and strength. That's when every other area of your life falls into place.

Make God first in your life. Read the Bible, His Word. Pray often. Go to church and get involved with other Christians. Most of all, fall in love with God again every single day.

LIFE LESSON

God loves us and wants us to love Him with all of our heart!

VERSE TO REMEMBER

What you should want most is God's kingdom and doing what he wants you to do. Then he will give you all these other things you need. MATTHEW 6:33 ERV

TO TALK ABOUT

Have you put God first in your life? How can you do that?

ABOUT THE AUTHOR

Mark Gilroy is the father of six children and coached them in several sports for 26 seasons. Mark loves sports and kids and believes there are many life skills and lessons that are developed by participating in athletics. He is a longtime publishing executive and has written six best-selling novels. He and his wife, Amy, reside in Brentwood, Tennessee.

LIVE YOUR FAITH

Dear Friend,

   This book was prayerfully crafted with you, the reader, in mind—every word, every sentence, every page—was thoughtfully written, designed, and packaged to encourage you...right where you are this very moment. At DaySpring, our vision is to see every person experience the life-changing message of God's love. So, as we worked through rough drafts, design changes, edits, and details, we prayed for you to deeply experience His unfailing love, indescribable peace, and pure joy. It is our sincere hope that through these Truth-filled pages your heart will be blessed, knowing that God cares about you—your desires and disappointments, your challenges and dreams.

He knows. He cares. He loves you unconditionally.

BLESSINGS!
THE DAYSPRING BOOK TEAM

Additional copies of this book and other DaySpring titles can be purchased at fine bookstores everywhere. Order online at <u>dayspring.com</u> or by phone at 1-877-751-4347